# Debugging

# Debugging

The Nine Indispensable Rules for Finding Even the
Most Elusive Software and Hardware Problems

**David J. Agans**

## AMACOM

### American Management Association

New York • Atlanta • Brussels • Buenos Aires • Chicago • London • Mexico City
San Francisco • Shanghai • Tokyo • Toronto • Washington, D.C.

Special discounts on bulk quantities of AMACOM books are available to corporations, professional associations, and other organizations. For details, contact Special Sales Department, AMACOM, a division of American Management Association, 1601 Broadway, New York, NY 10019.
Tel.: 212-903-8316. Fax: 212-903-8083.
Web site: www.amacombooks.org

This publication is designed to provide accurate and authoritative information in regard to the subject matter covered. It is sold with the understanding that the publisher is not engaged in rendering legal, accounting, or other professional service. If legal advice or other expert assistance is required, the services of a competent professional person should be sought.

Library of Congress Cataloging-in-Publication Data

Agans, David J., 1954–
    Debugging: the 9 indispensable rules for finding even the most elusive software and hardware problems / David J. Agans.
        p.   cm.
    Includes index.
    ISBN 0-8144-7457-8
    1. Debugging in computer science.   2. Computer software—Quality control.   I. Title.

QA76.9.D43 A35 2002
005.1' 4—dc21                                                    2002007990

To my mom, Ruth (Worsley) Agans, who debugged Fortran listings by hand at our dining room table, fueled by endless cups of strong coffee.

And to my dad, John Agans, who taught me to think, to use my common sense, and to laugh.

Your spirits are with me in all my endeavors.

# Contents

**Chapter 1: Introduction**                                        1
   How Can That Work?                                2
   Isn't It Obvious?                                 2
   Anyone Can Use It                                 3
   It'll Debug Anything                              4
   But It Won't Prevent, Certify, or Triage Anything    5
   More Than Just Troubleshooting                    6
   A Word About War Stories                          7
   Stay Tuned                                        8

**Chapter 2: The Rules—Suitable for Framing**                      9

**Chapter 3: Understand the System**                              11
   Read the Manual                                  13
   Read Everything, Cover to Cover                  15
   Know What's Reasonable                           17
   Know the Road Map                                18
   Know Your Tools                                  20
   Look It Up                                       21
   Remember                                         23
     *Understand the System*                23

**Chapter 4: Make It Fail**                                       25
   Do It Again                                      28
   Start at the Beginning                           29
   Stimulate the Failure                            29
   Don't Simulate the Failure                       30
   What If It's Intermittent?                       33

What if I've Tried Everything and It's Still
    Intermittent?                                                                35
    *A Hard Look at Bad Luck*                                                     35
    *Lies, Damn Lies, and Statistics*                                            37
    *Did You Fix It, or Did You Get Lucky?*                                       37
"But That Can't Happen"                                                           39
Never Throw Away a Debugging Tool                                                 41
Remember                                                                          42
    *Make It Fail*                                                                42

**Chapter 5: Quit Thinking and Look**                                            45
See the Failure                                                                   50
See the Details                                                                   52
Now You See It, Now You Don't                                                     55
Instrument the System                                                            55
    *Design Instrumentation In*                                                  56
    *Build Instrumentation In Later*                                              59
    *Don't Be Afraid to Dive In*                                                  60
    *Add Instrumentation On*                                                      61
    *Instrumentation in Daily Life*                                               62
The Heisenberg Uncertainty Principle                                             63
Guess Only to Focus the Search                                                   64
Remember                                                                          66
    *Quit Thinking and Look*                                                      66

**Chapter 6: Divide and Conquer**                                                67
Narrow the Search                                                                71
    *In the Ballpark*                                                             74
    *Which Side Are You On?*                                                      74
Inject Easy-to-Spot Patterns                                                     76
Start with the Bad                                                                78
Fix the Bugs You Know About                                                       79
Fix the Noise First                                                              80
Remember                                                                          80
    *Divide and Conquer*                                                          80

**Chapter 7: Change One Thing at a Time**                       83
  Use a Rifle, Not a Shotgun                                      85
  Grab the Brass Bar with Both Hands                              88
  Change One Test at a Time                                       89
  Compare with a Good One                                         90
  What Did You Change Since the Last Time It Worked?              92
  Remember                                                        95
    *Change One Thing at a Time*                         95

**Chapter 8: Keep an Audit Trail**                             97
  Write Down What You Did, in What Order, and
    What Happened                                        99
  The Devil Is in the Details                                    101
  Correlate                                                      103
  Audit Trails for Design Are Also Good for Testing             104
  The Shortest Pencil Is Longer Than the Longest
    Memory                                              105
  Remember                                                       106
    *Keep an Audit Trail*                                106

**Chapter 9: Check the Plug**                                  107
  Question Your Assumptions                                      109
  Don't Start at Square Three                                    111
  Test the Tool                                                  111
  Remember                                                       114
    *Check the Plug*                                     114

**Chapter 10: Get a Fresh View**                               115
  Ask for Help                                                   116
    *A Breath of Fresh Insight*                          116
    *Ask an Expert*                                      117
    *The Voice of Experience*                            117
  Where to Get Help                                              119
  Don't Be Proud                                                 120
  Report Symptoms, Not Theories                                  121
    *You Don't Have to Be Sure*                          122
  Remember                                                       123
    *Get a Fresh View*                                   123

**Chapter 11: If You Didn't Fix It, It Ain't Fixed**  125
Check That It's Really Fixed  127
Check That It's Really Your Fix That Fixed It  127
It Never Just Goes Away by Itself  128
Fix the Cause  129
Fix the Process  131
Remember  132
*If You Didn't Fix It, It Ain't Fixed*  132

**Chapter 12: All the Rules in One Story**  133

**Chapter 13: Easy Exercises for the Reader**  137
A Light Vacuuming Job  137
A Flock of Bugs  140
A Loose Restriction  144
The Jig Is Up  150

**Chapter 14: The View from the Help Desk**  157
Help Desk Constraints  159
The Rules, Help Desk Style  160
*Understand the System*  160
*Make It Fail*  162
*Quit Thinking and Look*  163
*Divide and Conquer*  164
*Change One Thing at a Time*  165
*Keep an Audit Trail*  166
*Check the Plug*  167
*Get a Fresh View*  167
*If You Didn't Fix It, It Ain't Fixed*  168
Remember  169
*The View from the Help Desk Is Murky*  169

**Chapter 15: The Bottom Line**  171
The Debugging Rules Web Site  171
If You're an Engineer  172
If You're a Manager  172
If You're a Teacher  173
Remember  174

**Index**  177

# Acknowledgments

This book was born in 1981 when a group of test technicians at Gould asked me if I could write a document on how to troubleshoot our hardware products. I was at a loss—the products were boards with hundreds of chips on them, several microprocessors, and numerous communications buses. I knew there was no magical recipe; they would just have to learn how to debug things. I discussed this with Mike Bromberg, a long time mentor of mine, and we decided the least we could do was write up some general rules of debugging. The Ten Debugging Commandments were the result, a single sheet of brief rules for debugging which quickly appeared on the wall above the test benches. Over the years, this list was compressed by one rule and generalized to software and systems, but it remains the core of this book. So to Mike, and to the floor techs who expressed the need, thanks.

Over the years, I've had the pleasure of working for and with a number of inspirational people who helped me develop both my debugging skills and my sense of humor. I'd like to recognize Doug Currie, Scott Ross, Glen Dash, Dick Morley, Mike Greenberg, Cos Fricano, John Aylesworth (one of the original techs), Bob DeSimone, and Warren Bayek for making challenging work a lot of fun. I should also mention three teachers who expected excellence and made learning enjoyable: Nick Menutti (it ain't the Nobel Prize, but here's your good word), Ray Fields, and Professor Francis F. Lee. And while

I never met them, their books have made a huge difference in my writing career: William Strunk Jr. and E. B. White (*The Elements of Style*), and Jeff Herman and Deborah Adams (*Write the Perfect Book Proposal*).

To the Delt Dawgs, my summer softball team of 28 years and counting, thanks for the reviews and networking help. I'm indebted to Charlie Seddon, who gave me a detailed review with many helpful comments, and to Bob Siedensticker, who did that and also gave me war stories, topic suggestions, and advice on the publishing biz. Several people, most of whom I did not know personally at the time, reviewed the book and sent me nice letters of endorsement, which helped get it published. Warren Bayek and Charlie Seddon (mentioned above), Dick Riley, Bob Oakes, Dave Miller, and Professor Terry Simkin: thank you for your time and words of encouragement.

I'm grateful to the Sesame Workshop, Tom and Ray Magliozzi (Click and Clack of *Car Talk*—or is it Clack and Click?), and Steve Martin for giving me permission to use their stories and jokes; to Sir Arthur Conan Doyle for creating Sherlock Holmes and having him make so many apropos comments; and to Seymour Friedel, Bob McIlvaine, and my brother Tom Agans for relating interesting war stories. And for giving me the examples I needed both to discover the rules and to demonstrate them, thanks to all the war story participants, both heroes and fools (you know who you are).

Working with my editors at Amacom has been a wonderful and enlightening experience. To Jacquie Flynn and Jim Bessent, thank you for your enthusiasm and great advice. And to the designers and other creative hands in the process, nice work; it came out great.

Special appreciation goes to my agent, Jodie Rhodes, for taking a chance on a first-time author with an offbeat approach to an unfamiliar subject. You know your markets, and it shows.

For their support, encouragement, and countless favors large and small, a special thanks to my in-laws, Dick and Joan Blagbrough. To my daughters, Jen and Liz, hugs and kisses for being fun and believing in me. (Also for letting me have a shot at the computer in the evenings between high-scoring games and instant messenger sessions.)

And finally, my eternal love and gratitude to my wife Gail, for encouraging me to turn the rules into a book, for getting me started on finding an agent, for giving me the time and space to write, and for proofreading numerous drafts that I wouldn't dare show anyone else. You can light up a chandelier with a vacuum cleaner, but you light up my life all by yourself.

Dave Agans
June 2002

# 1

---

# Introduction

"At present I am, as you know, fairly busy, but I propose to devote my declining years to the composition of a textbook which shall focus the whole art of detection into one volume."

—SHERLOCK HOLMES, *THE ADVENTURE OF THE ABBEY GRANGE*

This book tells you how to find out what's wrong with stuff, quick. It's short and fun because it *has* to be—if you're an engineer, you're too busy debugging to read anything more than the daily comics. Even if you're not an engineer, you often come across something that's broken, and you have to figure out how to fix it.

Now, maybe some of you never need to debug. Maybe you sold your dot.com IPO stock before the company went belly-up and you simply have your people look into the problem. Maybe you always luck out and your design just works—or, even less likely, the bug is always easy to find. But the odds are that you and all your competitors have a few hard-to-find bugs in your designs, and whoever fixes them quickest has an advantage. When you can find bugs fast, not only do you get quality products to customers quicker, you get yourself home earlier for quality time with your loved ones.

So put this book on your nightstand or in the bathroom, and in two weeks you'll be a debugging star.

## How Can That Work?

How can something that's so short and easy to read be so useful? Well, in my twenty-six years of experience designing and debugging systems, I've discovered two things (more than two, if you count stuff like "the first cup of coffee into the pot contains all the caffeine"):

1. When it took us a long time to find a bug, it was because we had neglected some essential, fundamental rule; once we applied the rule, we quickly found the problem.

2. People who excelled at quick debugging inherently understood and applied these rules. Those who struggled to understand or use these rules struggled to find bugs.

I compiled a list of these essential rules; I've taught them to other engineers and watched their debugging skill and speed increase. They really, really work.

## Isn't It Obvious?

As you read these rules, you may say to yourself, "But this is all so obvious." Don't be too hasty; these things *are* obvious (fundamentals usually are), but how they apply to a particular problem isn't always so obvious. And don't confuse obvious with easy—these rules aren't always easy to follow, and thus they're often neglected in the heat of battle.

The key is to *remember* them and *apply* them. If that was obvious and easy, I wouldn't have to keep reminding engineers to use them, and I wouldn't have a few dozen war stories about what happened when we didn't. Debuggers who naturally use these rules are hard to find. I like to ask job applicants, "What rules of thumb do you use when debugging?" It's amazing how many say, "It's an art." Great—we're going to have Picasso debugging our image-processing algorithm. The easy way and the artistic way do not find problems quickly.

This book takes these "obvious" principles and helps you remember them, understand their benefits, and know how to apply them, so you can resist the temptation to take a "shortcut" into what turns out to be a rat hole. It turns the art of debugging into a science.

Even if you're a very good debugger already, these rules will help you become even better. When an early draft of this book was reviewed by skilled debuggers, they had several comments in common: Besides teaching them one or two rules that they weren't already using (but would in the future), the book helped them crystallize the rules they already unconsciously followed. The team leaders (good debuggers rise to the top, of course) said that the book gave them the right words to transmit their skills to other members of the team.

## Anyone Can Use It

Throughout the book I use the term *engineer* to describe the reader, but the rules can be useful to a lot of you who may not consider yourselves engineers. Certainly, this includes you if you're involved in figuring out what's wrong with a design, whether your title is engineer, programmer, technician, customer support representative, or consultant.

If you're not directly involved in debugging, but you have responsibility for people who are, you can transmit the rules to your people. You don't even have to understand the details of the systems and tools your people use—the rules are fundamental, so after reading this book, even a pointy-haired manager should be able to help his far-more-intelligent teams find problems faster.

If you're a teacher, your students will enjoy the war stories, which will give them a taste of the real world. And when they burst onto that real world, they'll have a leg up on many of their more experienced (but untrained in debugging) competitors.

## It'll Debug Anything

This book is general; it's not about specific problems, specific tools, specific programming languages, or specific machines. Rather, it's about universal techniques that will help you to figure out any problem on any machine in any language using whatever tools you have. It's a whole new level of approach to the problem—for example, rather than tell you how to set the trigger on a Glitch-O-Matic digital logic analyzer, I'm going to tell you *why* you have to use an analyzer, even though it's a lot of trouble to hook it up.

It's also applicable to fixing all kinds of problems. Your system may have been designed wrong, built wrong, used wrong, or just plain got broken; in any case, these techniques will help you get to the heart of the problem quickly.

The methods presented here aren't even limited to engineering, although they were honed in the engineering environment. They'll help you figure out what's wrong with other things, like cars, houses, stereo equipment, plumbing, and human bodies. (There are examples in the book.) Admittedly, there are systems that resist these techniques—the economy is too complex, for example. And some systems don't need these methods; e.g., everybody already *knows* what's wrong with the government.

## But It Won't Prevent, Certify, or Triage Anything

While this book is general about methods and systems, it's very focused on *finding the causes of bugs and fixing them*.

It's not about quality development processes aimed at preventing bugs in the first place, such as ISO-9000, code reviews, or risk management. If you want to read about that, I recommend books like *The Tempura Method of Totalitarian Quality Management Processes* or *The Feng Shui Guide to Vermin-Free Homes*. Quality process techniques are valuable, but they're often not implemented; even when they are, they leave some bugs in the system.

Once you have bugs, you have to detect them; this takes place in your quality assurance (QA) department or, if you don't have one of those, at your customer site. This book doesn't deal with this stage either—test coverage analysis, test automation, and other QA techniques are well handled by other resources. A good book of poetry, such as *How Do I Test Thee, Let Me Count the Ways*, can help you while away the time as you check the 6,467,826 combinations of options in your product line.

And sooner or later, at least one of those combinations will fail, and some QA guy or customer is going to write up a bug report. Next, some managers, engineers, salespeople, and customer support people will probably get together in a triage meeting and argue passionately about how important the bug is, and therefore when and whether to fix it. This subject is deeply specific to your market, product, and resources, and this book will not touch it with a ten-foot pole. But when these people decide it has to be fixed, you'll have to look at the bug report and ask yourself, "How the heck did that happen?" That's when you use this book (see Figure 1-1).

The following chapters will teach you how to prepare to find a bug, dig up and sift through the clues to its cause, home in on the

Figure 1-1. When to Use This Book.

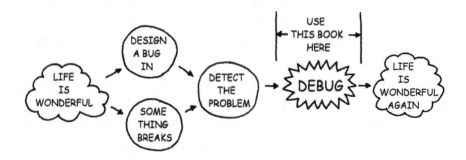

actual problem so you can fix it, and then make sure you really fixed it so you can go home triumphant.

## More Than Just Troubleshooting

Though the terms are often interchanged, there's a difference between debugging and troubleshooting, and there's a difference between this debugging book and the hundreds of troubleshooting guides available today. Debugging usually means figuring out why a design doesn't work as planned. Troubleshooting usually means figuring out what's broken in a particular copy of a product when the product's design is known to be good—there's a deleted file, a broken wire, or a bad part. Software engineers debug; car mechanics troubleshoot. Car *designers* debug (in an ideal world). Doctors troubleshoot the human body—they never got a chance to debug it. (It took God one day to design, prototype, and release that product; talk about schedule pressure! I guess we can forgive priority-two bugs like bunions and male pattern baldness.)

*The techniques in this book apply to both debugging and troubleshooting.* These techniques don't care how the problem got in there;

they just tell you how to find it. So they work whether the problem is a broken design or a broken part. Troubleshooting books, on the other hand, work *only* on a broken part. They boast dozens of tables, with symptoms, problems, and fixes for anything that might go wrong with a particular system. These *are* useful; they're a compendium of everything that has ever broken in that type of system, and what the symptoms and fixes were. They give a troubleshooter the experience of many others, and they help in finding known problems faster. But they don't help much with new, unknown problems. And thus they can't help with design problems, because engineers are so creative, they like to make up new bugs, not use the same old ones.

So if you're troubleshooting a standard system, don't ignore Rule 8 ("Get a Fresh View"); go ahead and consult a troubleshooting guide to see if your problem is listed. But if it isn't, or if the fix doesn't work, or if there's no troubleshooting guide out yet because you're debugging the world's first digital flavor transmission system, you won't have to worry, because the rules in this book will get you to the heart of your brand-new problem.

## A Word About War Stories

I'm a male American electronics engineer, born in 1954. When I tell a "war story" about some problem that got solved somehow, it's a real story, so it comes from things that male American electronics engineers born in 1954 know about. You may not be all or any of those, so you may not understand some of the things I mention. If you're an auto mechanic, you may not know what an interrupt is. If you were born in 1985, you may not know what a record player is. No matter; the principle being demonstrated is still worth knowing, and I'll explain enough as I go along so you'll be able to get the principle.

You should also know that I've taken some license with the details to protect the innocent, and especially the guilty.

## Stay Tuned

In this book I'll introduce the nine golden rules of debugging, then devote a chapter to each. I'll start each chapter with a war story where the rule proved crucial to success; then I'll describe the rule and show how it applies to the story. I'll discuss various ways of thinking about and using the rule that are easy to remember in the face of complex technological problems (or even simple ones). And I'll give you some variations showing how the rule applies to other stuff like cars and houses.

In the final few chapters, I've included a set of war stories to exercise your understanding, a section on using the rules under the trying circumstances of the help desk, and a few last hints for putting what you've learned to work in your job.

When you're done with this book, your debugging efficiency will be much higher than before. You may even find yourself wandering around, looking for engineers in distress so you can swoop in and save the day. One bit of advice, though: Leave the leotard and cape at home.

# 2

# The Rules–Suitable for Framing

"The theories which I have expressed there, and which appear to you to be so chimerical, are really extremely practical—so practical that I depend upon them for my bread and cheese."

—SHERLOCK HOLMES, *A STUDY IN SCARLET*

Here is a list of the rules. Memorize them. Tape them to your wall. Tape them to all of your walls. (Coming soon: Debugging Rules wallpaper, for the seriously decor-challenged home office; definitely *not* recommended by feng shui experts.)

# ☞ DEBUGGING RULES ☜

### Understand the System

### Make It Fail

### Quit Thinking and Look

### Divide and Conquer

### Change One Thing at a Time

### Keep an Audit Trail

### Check the Plug

### Get a Fresh View

### If You Didn't Fix It, It Ain't Fixed

© 2001 David Agans                    www.debuggingrules.com

# 3

# Understand the System

"It is not so impossible, however, that a man should possess all knowledge which is likely to be useful to him in his work, and this, I have endeavoured in my case to do."

—SHERLOCK HOLMES, *THE FIVE ORANGE PIPS*

**War Story.** When I was just out of college and trying to get experience (among other things), I took on a moonlighting job building a microprocessor-based valve controller. The device was designed to control the amount of metal powder going into a mold, and it took measurements from a scale that weighed the powder (see Figure 3-1). As many engineers do (especially still-wet-behind-the-ears engineers), I copied the basic design (from a frat brother who had used the same processor chip in his thesis project).

But my design didn't work. When the scale tried to interrupt the processor with a new measurement, the processor ignored it. Since I was moonlighting, I didn't have many tools for debugging, so it took me a long time to figure out that the chip that got the interrupt signal from the scale wasn't passing it on to the processor.

I was working with a software guy, and at one o'clock in the morning, very frustrated, he insisted that I get out the data book and read it, front to back. I

Figure 3-1. A Microprocessor-Based Valve Controller.

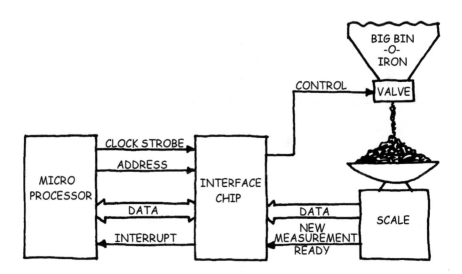

did, and there on page 37, I read, "The chip will interrupt the microprocessor on the first deselected clock strobe." This is like saying the interrupt will happen the first time the phone rings, but the call isn't for the chip—which would never happen in my design, since I (like my frat brother) had saved some hardware by combining the clock with the address lines. To continue with the phone analogy, the phone rang *only* when the call *was* for the chip. My frat brother's system didn't have any interrupts, however, so his worked. Once I added the extra hardware, so did mine.

Later, I described my marathon debugging effort to my dad (who knew little about electronics, and nothing about microprocessors). He said, "That's just common sense—when all else fails, read the instructions." This gave me my first inkling that there are general rules of debugging that can apply to more than just computers and software. (I also realized that even a college education wasn't enough to impress my dad.) In this case, the rule was "Understand the System." ▨

I couldn't begin to debug the problem until I understood how the chip worked. As soon as I did understand it, the problem was obvious. Bear in mind that I understood much of the system, and that was important; I knew how my design worked, that the scale had to interrupt the processor, and what clock strobes and address lines do. But I didn't look closely at everything, and I got burned.

You need a working knowledge of what the system is supposed to do, how it's designed, and, in some cases, why it was designed that way. If you don't understand some part of the system, that always seems to be where the problem is. (This is not just Murphy's Law; if you don't understand it when you design it, you're more likely to mess up.)

By the way, understanding the system doesn't mean understanding the problem—that's like Steve Martin's foolproof method for becoming a millionaire: "First, get a million dollars. . . ."* Of course you don't understand the problem yet, but you have to understand how things are supposed to work if you want to figure out why they don't.

## Read the Manual

The essence of "Understand the System" is, "Read the manual." Contrary to my dad's comment, read it first—*before* all else fails. When you buy something, the manual tells you what you're supposed to do to it, and how it's supposed to act as a result. You need to read this from cover to cover and understand it in order to get the results you want. Sometimes you'll find that it *can't* do what you want—you bought the wrong thing. So, contrary to my earlier opinion, read the manual before you *buy* the useless piece of junk.

If your lawn mower doesn't start, reading the manual might remind you to squeeze the primer bulb a few times before pulling the rope. We have a weed whacker that used to get so hot it would fuse

*Included by permission of Steve Martin.

the trimmer lines together and they wouldn't feed out any more; the yardwork kid who set it up had neglected to read the part of the manual that covered lubricating the trimmer head. I figured it out by reading the manual. If that tofu casserole came out awful, reread the recipe. (Actually, in the case of tofu casserole, getting the recipe right might not help; you'll be better off reading the take-out menu from the Chu-Quik Chou House.)

If you're an engineer debugging something your company made, you need to read your internal manual. What did your engineers design it to do? Read the functional specification. Read any design specs; study schematics, timing diagrams, and state machines. Study their code, and read the comments. (Ha! Ha! Read the *comments!* Get it?) Do design reviews. Figure out what the engineers who built it expected it to do, besides make them rich enough to buy a Beemer.

A caution here: Don't necessarily trust this information. Manuals (and engineers with Beemers in their eyes) can be wrong, and many a difficult bug arises from this. But you still need to know what they thought they built, even if you have to take that information with a bag of salt.

And sometimes, this information is just what you need to see:

**War Story.** We were debugging an embedded firmware program that was coded in assembly language. This meant we were dealing directly with the microprocessor registers. We found that the B register was getting clobbered, and we narrowed down the problem to a call into a subroutine. As we looked at the source code for the subroutine, we found the following comment at the top: "/* Caution—this subroutine clobbers the B register. */" Fixing the routine so that it left the B register alone fixed the bug. (Of course, it would have been easier for the original engineer to save the B register than to type the comment, but at least it was documented.)

At another company, we were looking at a situation where things seemed to be happening in the wrong order. We looked at the source code, which I had written some time previously, and I said to my associate that I remembered being worried about such a thing at one time. We did a text search for "bug" and found the following comment above two function calls: "/* DJA—Bug here? Maybe should call these in reverse order? */" Indeed, calling the two functions in the reverse order fixed the bug. ■

There's a side benefit to understanding your own systems, too. When you do find the bugs, you'll need to fix them without breaking anything else. Understanding what the system is supposed to do is the first step toward not breaking it.

## Read Everything, Cover to Cover

It's very common for people to try to debug something without *thoroughly* reading the manual for the system they're using. They've skimmed it, looking at the sections they thought were important, but the section they didn't read held the clue to what was wrong. Heck, that's how I ended up struggling with that valve controller at one o'clock in the morning.

Programming guides and APIs can be very thick, but you have to dig in—the function that you assume you understand is the one that bites you. The parts of the schematic that you ignore are where the noise is coming from. That little line on the data sheet that specifies an obscure timing parameter can be the one that matters.

**War Story.** We built several versions of a communications board, some with three telephone circuits installed and some with four. The three-wide systems had been working fine in the field for a while when we introduced the four-wides at a beta site. We had given these systems less internal testing, since the circuits were identical to the proven three-wides—there was just one more circuit installed.

The four-wides failed under high temperature at the beta site. We quickly re-created the failures in our lab and found that the main processor had crashed. This often means bad program memory, so we ran tests and found that memory was reading back incorrectly. We wondered why the identical three-wide boards didn't have this problem.

The hardware designer looked at a few boards and noticed that the memory chips on the four-wides were a different brand (they were built in a different lot). He looked at the specs: Both chips were approved by engineering, both were very fast, and they had identical timing for read and write access. The designer had correctly accounted for these specs in the processor timing.

I read the whole data sheet. The one spec that was different on the bad memories defined how long you had to wait *between* accesses. The amount of time seemed short and insignificant, and the difference between the wait times for the two memories was even less, but the processor timing design had *not* accounted for it and didn't meet the spec for either chip. So it failed often on the slower chip, and it probably would have failed on the faster chip sooner or later.

We fixed the problem by slowing the processor down a little, and the next revision of the design used faster memories and accounted for every line of the data sheet. ▪

Application notes and implementation guides provide a wealth of information, not only about how something works, but specifically about problems people have had with it before. Warnings about common mistakes are incredibly valuable (even if you make only uncommon mistakes). Get the latest documentation from the vendor's Web site, and read up on this week's common mistakes.

Reference designs and sample programs tell you one way to use a product, and sometimes this is all the documentation you get. Be careful with such designs, however; they are often created by people who know their product but don't follow good design practices, or don't design for real-world applications. (Lack of error recovery is the most popular shortcut.) Don't just lift the design; you'll find the bugs in it later if you don't find them at first. Also, even the best reference design probably won't match the specifics of your application, and that's where it breaks. It happened to me when I lifted my frat brother's microprocessor design—his didn't work with interrupts.

## Know What's Reasonable

When you're looking around in a system, you have to know how the system would normally work. If you don't know that low-order bytes come first in Intel-based PC programs, you're going to think that all your longwords got scrambled. If you don't know what cache does, you'll be very confused by memory writes that don't seem to "take" right away. If you don't understand how a tri-state data bus works, you'll think those are mighty glitchy signals on that board. If you've never heard a chain saw, you might think the problem has something to do with that godawful loud buzzing noise. Knowledge of what's normal helps you notice things that aren't.

You have to know a little bit about the fundamentals of your technical field. If I hadn't known what clock strobes and address lines did, I wouldn't have understood the interrupt problem even after I read the manual. Almost all, if not all, of the examples in this book involve people who knew *some* fundamentals about how the systems worked. (And let me apologize now if I've somehow led you to believe that reading this book will allow you to walk into any technological situation and figure out the bugs. If you're a games programmer, you probably ought to steer clear of debugging nuclear power plants.

If you're not a doctor, don't try to diagnose that gray-green splotch on your arm. And if you're a politician, please, don't mess with *any-thing*.)

**War Story.** A software engineer I worked with came out of a debugging strategy meeting shaking his head in disbelief. The bug was that the microprocessor would crash. It was just a little micro—no operating system, no virtual memory, no anything else; the only way they knew it had crashed was that it stopped resetting a watchdog timer, which eventually timed out. The software guys were trying to figure out where it was crashing. One of the hardware guys suggested they "put in a breakpoint just *before* the crash, and when the breakpoint hits, look around at what's happening." Apparently, he didn't really understand cause and effect—if they knew where to put the breakpoint, they would have found the problem already.

This is why hardware and software people get on each other's nerves when they try to debug each other's stuff. ▪

Lack of fundamental understanding explains why so many people have trouble figuring out what's wrong with their home computer: They just don't understand the fundamentals about computers. If you can't learn what you need to, you just have to follow debugging Rule 8 and Get a Fresh View from someone with more expertise or experience. The teenager across the street will do nicely. And have him fix the flashing "12:00" on your VCR while he's around.

## Know the Road Map

When you're trying to navigate to where a bug is hiding, you have to know the lay of the land. Initial guesses about where to divide a system in order to isolate the problem depend on your knowing what functions are where. You need to understand, at least at the top level, what all the blocks and all the interfaces do. If the toaster oven burns the toast, you need to know that the darkness knob controls the toasting time.

You should know what goes across all the APIs and communication interfaces in your system. You should know what each module or program is supposed to do with what it receives and transmits through those interfaces. If your code is very modular or object oriented, the interfaces will be simple and the modules well defined. It'll be easy to look at the interfaces and interpret whether what you're seeing is correct.

When there are parts of the system that are "black boxes," meaning that you don't know what's inside them, knowing how they're supposed to interact with other parts allows you to at least locate the problem as being inside the box or outside the box. If the problem is inside the box, you have to replace the box, but if it's outside, you can fix it. To use the burnt toast example, you have control of the darkness knob, so you try turning the knob to lighter, and if that doesn't shorten the toasting time, you assume that the problem is inside the toaster, throw it out, and get a new one. (Or you take it apart and try to fix it, then throw it out and get a new one.)

Suppose you're driving your car and you hear a "tap-tap-tap" sound that seems to go faster as you drive faster. There could be a rock in the tire tread (easy to fix), or maybe something is wrong in the engine (hard to fix); at highway speeds, the engine and the tires speed up and slow down together. But if you understand that the engine is connected to the tires through the transmission, you know that if you downshift, the engine will go faster for the same tire speed. So you downshift, and when the sound stays the same, you figure the problem is in the tire, pull over, and find the rock in the tread. Except for the transmission job you'll need because you downshifted at highway speeds, you've saved yourself an expensive trip to the repair shop.

## Know Your Tools

Your debugging tools are your eyes and ears into the system; you have to be able to choose the right tool, use the tool correctly, and interpret the results you get properly. (If you stick the wrong end of the thermometer under your tongue, it won't read the right temperature.) Many tools have very powerful features that only a well-versed user knows about. The more well versed you are, the easier it will be for you to see what's going on in your system. Take the time to learn everything you can about your tools—often, the key to seeing what's going on (see Rule 3, Quit Thinking and Look) is how well you set up your debugger or trigger your analyzer.

You also have to know the limitations of your tools. Stepping through source code shows logic errors but not timing or multithread problems; profiling tools can expose timing problems but not logic flaws. Analog scopes can see noise but can't store much data; digital logic analyzers catch lots of data but can't see noise. A health thermometer can't tell if the taffy is too hot, and a candy thermometer isn't accurate enough to measure a fever.

The hardware guy who suggested a breakpoint before the crash didn't know the limitations of breakpoints (or he had some fancy time-travel technique up his sleeve). What the software guy eventually did was hook up a logic analyzer to record a trace of the address and data buses of the micro and set the watchdog timer to a very short time; when it timed out, he saved the trace. He knew he had to record what was happening, since he wouldn't know that the micro had crashed until the timer triggered. He shortened the timer because he knew the analyzer could remember only so much data before it would forget the older stuff. He was able to see when the program jumped into the weeds by looking at the trace.

You also have to know your development tools. This includes, of course, the language you're writing software in—if you don't know what the "+ =" operator does in C, you're going to screw up the code somewhere. But it also involves knowing more subtle things about what the compiler and linker do with your source code before the machine sees it. How data is aligned, references are handled, and memory is allocated will affect your program in ways that aren't obvious from looking at the source program. Hardware engineers have to know how a definition in a high-level chip design language will be translated into registers and gates on the chip.

# Look It Up

**War Story.** A junior engineer (we'll call him "Junior") working for a large computer manufacturer was designing a system that included a chip called a 1489A. This chip receives signals from a communication wire, like the kind between a computer and a telephone Internet modem. One of the senior engineers (we'll call him "Kneejerk") saw the design and said, "Oh, you shouldn't use a 1489A. You should use the old 1489." Junior asked why, and Kneejerk replied, "Because the 1489A gets really hot." Well, being suspicious of all older people, as brash young folk tend to be, Junior decided to try to understand the circuit and figure out why the new version of the chip got hot. He found that the only difference between the two chips was the value of an internal bias resistor, which made the new part more immune to noise on the wire. Now, this resistor *was* smaller in the 1489A, so if you applied lots of voltage to it, it would get hotter; but the resistor was connected in such a way that it couldn't get much voltage—certainly not enough to get hot. Thus understanding the circuit, Junior ignored Kneejerk's advice and used the part. It did not get hot.

A few months later, Junior was looking at a circuit that had been designed by the group previously. As he put his scope probe down on what the diagram said was the input pin of the old 1489 they had used, the pin number didn't seem right. He looked it up in his well-worn data book, and sure enough, they had gotten the pinout wrong and connected the input to a bias pin instead of the input pin. The bias pin is generally supposed to be unconnected, but if you hook the input up to it, it sort of works, though the part has no noise immunity at all. This misconnection also happens to bypass an input resistor and make the part draw a lot of current through the internal bias resistor. In fact, Junior noted with amusement, it gets hot, and it would get hotter if you used a 1489A. ▦

Two parts of the "Understand the System" rule were violated here. First, when they designed the circuit, the original engineers didn't look up the pin numbers to make sure they had the right ones. Then, to complicate matters, Kneejerk didn't try to understand the circuit and figure out why the newer part got hot. The truly sad thing is that, as a result, this team had been designing circuits with old, hard-to-get parts that ran far too hot and had no noise immunity at all. Other than that, they did great work.

Junior, on the other hand, didn't trust the schematic diagram pinout and looked up the correct one in the data book. *He* figured out why the part got hot.

Don't guess. Look it up. Detailed information has been written down somewhere, either by you or by someone who manufactured a chip or wrote a software utility, and you shouldn't trust your memory about it. Pinouts of chips, parameters for functions, or even function names—look them up. Be like Einstein, who never remembered his own phone number. "Why bother?" he would ask. "It's in the phone book."

If you make guesses when you go to look at a signal on a chip, you may end up looking at the wrong signal, which may look right. If you assume that the parameters to a function call are in the right order, you may skip past the problem just like the original designer did. You may get confusing information or, even worse, falsely reassuring information. Don't waste your debugging time looking at the wrong stuff.

Finally, for the sake of humanity, if you can't fix the flood in your basement at 2 A.M. and decide to call the plumber, don't guess the number. Look it up.

## Remember

### Understand the System

This is the first rule because it's the most important. Understand?

- **Read the manual.** It'll tell you to lubricate the trimmer head on your weed whacker so that the lines don't fuse together.

- **Read everything in depth.** The section about the interrupt getting to your microcomputer is buried on page 37.

- **Know the fundamentals.** Chain saws are *supposed* to be loud.

- **Know the road map.** Engine speed can be different from tire speed, and the difference is in the transmission.

- **Understand your tools.** Know which end of the thermometer is which, and how to use the fancy features on your Glitch-O-Matic logic analyzer.

- **Look up the details.** Even Einstein looked up the details. Kneejerk, on the other hand, trusted his memory.

chapter

# 4

# Make It Fail

"There is nothing like first-hand evidence."

—SHERLOCK HOLMES, *A STUDY IN SCARLET*

**War Story.** In 1975, I was alone in the lab late one night (it's always late at night, isn't it?) trying to solve a problem on a TV pong game, one of the first home TV games, which was being developed at the MIT Innovation Center with funding from a local entrepreneur. We had a practice-wall feature, and the bug I was trying to solve happened occasionally when the ball bounced off the practice wall. I set up my oscilloscope (the thing that makes squiggles on a little round screen in old sci-fi movies) and watched for the bug, but I found it very difficult to watch the scope properly—if I set the ball speed too slow, it bounced off the wall only once every few seconds, and if I set it too fast, I had to give all my attention to hitting the ball back to the wall. If I missed, I'd have to wait until the next ball was launched in order to see the bug. This was not a very efficient way to debug, and I thought to myself, "Well, it's only a game." No, actually, what I thought was that it would be great if I could make it play by itself.

It turned out that the up/down position of the paddles and the position of the ball in both directions (up/down and left/right) were represented by voltages (see Figure 4-1). (For you nonhardware types, a voltage is like the level of water

Figure 4-1. TV Tennis.

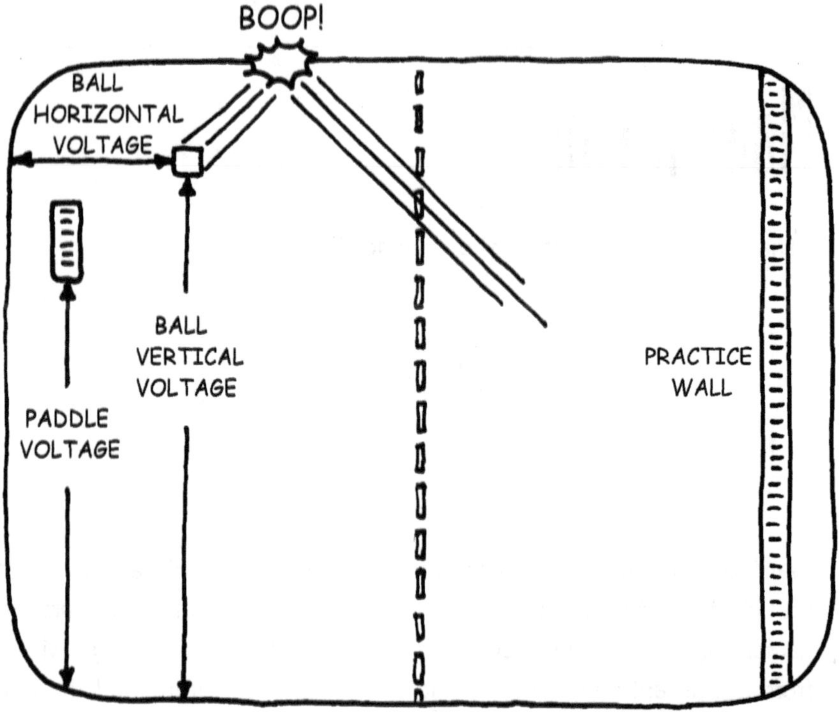

in a tank; you fill and empty the tank to change the level. Except that it's not water, it's electrons.)

I realized that if I connected the paddle voltage to the up/down voltage of the ball instead of to the hand controller, the paddle would follow the ball up and down. Whenever the ball got to the side, the paddle would be at the right height to hit it back toward the wall. I hooked it up this way, and my ghost player was very good indeed. With the game merrily playing itself, I was able to keep my eyes on the scope and proceeded to find and fix my problem quickly. ■

Even late at night, I could easily see what was wrong once I could watch the scope while the circuit failed. Getting it to fail while I

watched was the key. This is typical of many debugging problems—
you can't see what's going on because it doesn't happen when it's
convenient to look at it. And that doesn't mean it happens only late
at night (though that's when you end up debugging it)—it may happen only one out of seven times, or it happened that one time when
Charlie was testing it.

Now, if Charlie were working at my company, and you asked
him, "What do you do when you find a failure?" he would answer,
"Try to make it fail again." (Charlie is well trained.) There are three
reasons for trying to make it fail:

- **So you can look at it.** In order to see it fail (and we'll discuss
  this more in the next section), you have to be able to make it
  fail. You have to make it fail as regularly as possible. In my TV
  game situation, I was able to keep my bleary eyes on the scope
  at the moments the problem occurred.

- **So you can focus on the cause.** Knowing under exactly what
  conditions it will fail helps you focus on probable causes. (But
  be careful; sometimes this is misleading—for example, "The
  toast burns only if you put bread in the toaster; therefore the
  problem is with the bread." We'll discuss more about guessing
  later.)

- **So you can tell if you've fixed it.** Once you think you've fixed
  the problem, having a surefire way to make it fail gives you a
  surefire test of whether you fixed it. If without the fix it fails
  100 percent of the time when you do X, and with the fix it fails
  zero times when you do X, you know you've really fixed the
  bug. (This is not silly. Many times an engineer will change the
  software to fix a bug, then test the new software under different
  conditions from those that exposed the bug. It would have
  worked even if he had typed limericks into the code, but he
  goes home happy. And weeks later, in testing or, worse, at the
  customer site, it fails again. More on this later, too.)

**War Story.** I recently purchased a vehicle with all-wheel-drive and drove it all summer with no problems. When the bitter cold weather set in (in New Hampshire, that's usually sometime in September), I noticed that there was a whining noise coming from the rear of the car for the first few minutes if the speed was between 25 and 30 mph. At faster or slower speeds, it would go away. After 10 minutes, it would go away. If the temperature was warmer than 25 degrees, it would go away.

I took the vehicle in to the dealer for some regular maintenance, and I asked them to take it out first thing in the morning if it was cold and listen for the sound. They didn't get to it until 11 A.M., when the temperature was 37 degrees—it didn't make a sound. They removed the wheels and looked for problems in the brakes and found nothing (of course). They hadn't made it fail, so they had no chance of finding the problem. (I've been trying to get the car there on another cold day, and we have had the warmest winter in history in New Hampshire. This is Murphy's Law. I think the weather will turn cold again once the car's warranty has run out.) ▦

## Do It Again

But how do you make it fail? Well, one easy way is to demo it on a trade-show floor; just as effective is to show it to prospective investors. If you don't happen to have any customers or investors handy, you'll have to make do with using the device normally and watching for it to do the wrong thing. This is what testing is all about, of course, but the important part is to be able to make it fail again, *after* the first time. A well-documented test procedure is always a plus, but mainly you just have to have the attitude that one failure is not enough. When a three-year-old watches her father fall off the stepladder and flip the paint can upside down onto his head, she claps and says, "Do it again!" Act like a three-year-old.

Look at what you did and do it again. Write down each step as you go. Then follow your own written procedure to make sure it really causes the error. (Fathers with paint cans on their heads are excused from this last exercise. In fact, there *are* situations where making a device fail is destructive or otherwise painful, and in these cases making it fail the same way every time is not good. You have to change something to limit the damage, but you should try to change as little of the original system and sequence as possible.)

## Start at the Beginning

Often the steps required are short and few: Just click on this icon and the misspelled message appears. Sometimes the sequence is simple, but there's a lot of setup required: Just reboot the computer, start these five programs, and *then* click on this icon and the misspelled message appears. Because bugs can depend on a complex state of the machine, you have to be careful to note the state of the machine going into your sequence. (If you tell the mechanic that your car windows stick closed whenever you drive in cold weather, he probably ought to know that you take it through the car wash every morning.) Try to start the sequence from a known state, such as a freshly rebooted computer or the car when you first walk into the garage.

## Stimulate the Failure

When the failure sequence requires a lot of manual steps, it can be helpful to automate the process. This is exactly what I did in my TV game example; I needed to play and debug at the same time, and the automatic paddle took care of playing. (Too bad I couldn't automate the debugging part and just play!) In many cases, the failure occurs

only after a large number of repetitions, so you want to run an automated tester all night. Software is happy to work all night, and you
don't even have to buy it pizza.

**War Story.** My house had a window that leaked only when it rained hard and
the wind was from the southeast. I didn't wait for the next big storm; I got out
there with a ladder and a hose and made it leak. This allowed me to see exactly
where the water was getting in, determine that there was a gap in the caulking,
and, after I caulked it, verify that even under hose pressure the leak was fixed. ▨

An allergist will prick your skin with various allergens in a known
pattern to see which ones cause a reaction. A dentist will spray cold
air over your teeth to find the cold-sensitive spot. (Also, dentists do
this just for fun.) And a state trooper will make you walk a straight
line, lean back and touch your nose, and recite the alphabet backward to determine whether you're alcohol impaired (this is a lot safer
than letting you drive a little farther to see if you can stay on your
side of the highway).

If your Web server software is grabbing the wrong Web page occasionally, set up a Web browser to ask for pages automatically. If
your network software gets errors under high-traffic conditions, run
a network-loading tool to simulate the load, and thus stimulate the
failure.

## Don't Simulate the Failure

There's a big difference between *stimulating* the failure (good) and
*simulating* the failure (not good). In the previous example, I recommended simulating the network load, not simulating the failure

mechanism itself. *Simulating* the *conditions* that *stimulate* the *failure* is okay. But try to avoid simulating the failure mechanism itself.

"Why would I do that?" you might ask. Well, if you have an intermittent bug, you might guess that a particular low-level mechanism was causing the failure, build a configuration that exercises that low-level mechanism, and then look for the failure to happen a lot. Or, you might deal with a bug found offsite by trying to set up an equivalent system in your own lab. In either case, you're trying to *simulate* the failure—i.e., to re-create it, but in a different way or on a different system.

In cases where you guess at the failure mechanism, simulation is often unsuccessful. Usually, either because the guess was wrong or because the test changes the conditions, your simulated system will work flawlessly all the time or, worse, fail in a new way that distracts you from the original bug you were looking for. Your word-processing application (the one you're going to knock off Microsoft with) is dropping paragraphs, and you guess that it has something to do with writing out the file. So you build a test program that writes to the disk constantly, and the operating system locks up. You conclude that the problem is that Windows is too slow and proceed to develop a new Microsoft-killing operating system.

You have enough bugs already; don't try to create new ones. Use instrumentation to look at what's going wrong (see Rule 3: Quit Thinking and Look), but don't change the mechanism; that's what's causing the failure. In the word processor example, rather than changing how things get written to the disk, it would be better to automatically generate keystrokes and watch what gets written to the disk.

Simulating a bug by trying to re-create it on a similar system is more useful, within limits. If a bug can be re-created on more than one system, you can characterize it as a design bug—it's not just the one system that's broken in some way. Being able to re-create it on some configurations and not on others helps you narrow down the possible causes. But if you can't re-create it quickly, don't start modifying your simulation to get it to happen. You'll be creating new configurations, not looking at a copy of the one that failed. When you have a system that fails in any kind of regular manner, even intermittently, go after the problem on *that* system in *that* configuration.

The typical situation is an integration problem at a customer site: Your software fails in a particular machine when it's driving a particular peripheral device. You may be able to simulate the failure at your site by setting up the same configuration. But if you don't have the same equipment or the same conditions, and thus the software doesn't fail, the temptation is to try to simulate the equipment or invent new test programs. Don't do it—bite the bullet and either bring the equipment to your engineers or send an engineer to the equipment (with a taxi-load of instrumentation). If your customer site is in Aruba, you'll probably reject the "bring the equipment in" option out of hand—and, by the way, are you currently hiring experienced engineers with good writing and debugging skills?

The red flag to watch out for is substituting a seemingly identical environment and expecting it to fail in the same way. It's not identical. When I was trying to fix my leaky window, if I had assumed that the problem was a faulty window design, I might have tested it using another "exactly the same" window. And I wouldn't have found the gap in the caulking, which was particular to the window that was failing.

Q: How many engineers does it take to fix a lightbulb?

A: None; they all say, "I can't reproduce it—the lightbulb in *my* office works fine."

Remember, this doesn't mean you shouldn't automate or amplify your testing in order to *stimulate* the failure. Automation can make an intermittent problem happen much more quickly, as in the TV game story. Amplification can make a subtle problem much more obvious, as in the leaky window example, where I could locate the leak better with a hose than with the occasional rainstorm. Both of these techniques help stimulate the failure, without simulating the mechanism that's failing. Make your changes at a high enough level that they don't affect how the system fails, just how often.

Also, watch out that you don't overdo it and cause new problems. Don't be the hardware guy who assumes that the problem is heat related and blows a hot-air gun on the chip until it melts, then decides that the bug is all this goopy melted plastic on the circuit board. If I had used a fire hose to test for the leak, I might have concluded that the problem was obviously the shattered window.

## What If It's Intermittent?

"Make it Fail" gets a lot harder when the failure happens only once in a while. And many tough problems are intermittent, which is why we don't always apply this rule—it's hard to apply. You may know exactly how you made it fail the first time, but it still fails in only 1 out of 5, or 1 out of 10, or (gulp) 1 out of 450 tries.

The key here is that you don't know exactly how you made it fail. You know exactly what you did, but you don't know all of the exact conditions. There were other factors that you didn't notice or couldn't control—initial conditions, input data, timing, outside processes, electrical noise, temperature, vibration, network traffic, phase of the moon, and sobriety of the tester. If you can get control of all those conditions, you will be able to make it happen all the time. Of course, sometimes you can't control them, and we'll discuss that in the next section.

What can you do to control these other conditions? First of all, figure out what they are. In software, look for uninitialized data (tsk, tsk!), random data input, timing variations, multithread synchronization, and outside devices (like the phone network or the six thousand kids clicking on your Web site). In hardware, look for noise, vibration, temperature, timing, and parts variations (type or vendor). In my all-wheel-drive example, the problem would have seemed intermittent if I hadn't noticed the temperature and the speed.

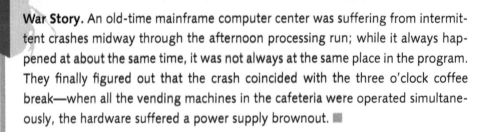

**War Story.** An old-time mainframe computer center was suffering from intermittent crashes midway through the afternoon processing run; while it always happened at about the same time, it was not always at the same place in the program. They finally figured out that the crash coincided with the three o'clock coffee break—when all the vending machines in the cafeteria were operated simultaneously, the hardware suffered a power supply brownout. ■

Once you have an idea of what conditions might be affecting the system, you simply have to try a lot of variations. Initialize those arrays and put a known pattern into the inputs of your erratic software. Try to control the timing and then vary it to see if you can get the system to fail at a particular setting. Shake, heat, chill, inject noise into, and tweak the clock speed and the power supply voltage of that unreliable circuit board until you see some change in the frequency of failure.

Sometimes you'll find that controlling a condition makes the problem go away. You've discovered something—what condition, when random, is causing the failure. If this happens, of course, you want to try every possible value of that condition until you hit the one that causes the system to fail. Try every possible input data pattern if a random one fails occasionally and a controlled one doesn't.

Sometimes you'll find that you can't really control a condition, but you can make it more random—vibrating a circuit board, for example, or injecting noise. If the problem is intermittent because the failure is caused by a low-likelihood event (such as a noise peak), then making the condition (the noise) more random increases the likelihood of these events. The error will occur more often. This may be the best you can do, and it helps a lot—it tells you what condition causes the failure, and it gives you a better chance of seeing the failure while it's happening. One caution: Watch out that the amplified condition isn't just causing a new error. If a board has a temperature-sensitive error and you decide to vibrate it until all the chips come loose, you'll get more errors, but they won't have anything to do with the original problem.

Sometimes, nothing seems to make any difference, and you're back where you started. It's still intermittent.

## What If I've Tried Everything and It's Still Intermittent?

Remember that there are three reasons to make it fail: so you can look at it, so you can get a clue about the cause, and so you can tell when it's fixed. Here's how to accomplish those goals even when the blasted thing seems to have a mind of its own. Because, remember, it doesn't have a mind of its own—the failure has a cause, and you can find it. It's just really well hidden behind a lot of random factors that you haven't been able to unrandomize.

### A Hard Look at Bad Luck

You have to be able to look at the failure. If it doesn't happen every time, you have to *look at it each time it fails, while ignoring the many times it doesn't fail.* The key is to *capture information on every run so you can look at it after you know that it's failed.* Do this by having the system output as much information as possible while it's running and recording this information in a "debug log" file.

By looking at captured information, you can easily compare a bad run to a good one (see Rule 5: Change One Thing at a Time). If you capture the right information, you *will* be able to see some difference between a good case and a failure case. Note carefully the things that happen only in the failure cases. This is what you look at when you actually start to debug.

Even though the failure is intermittent, this lets you identify and capture the cases where it occurs and work on them as if they happened every time.

**War Story.** We had an intermittent videoconferencing problem when our unit called a certain other vendor's unit. In one out of five calls, the other system would shut down the video and go into a simple audio phone call.

We couldn't look inside the other system, but we did take debug logs of ours. We captured two calls, one right after the other, where the first one worked and the second one didn't. In the log of the call that failed was a message that said we were sending a surprise command over the wire. We checked the good call, then other good calls, and it never happened in them. We took more logs until we got a bad call again, and sure enough, there in the bad log was the surprise command.

It turned out that there was a memory buffer full of old commands from the previous call that might not get emptied out before a new call started sending commands. If the buffer got emptied out, everything worked okay. If it didn't, the rogue command that we saw was sent at the beginning of the call, and the other vendor's unit would misinterpret it and go into the simple audio mode.

We could see this system fail because we tracked enough information on every call. Even though the failure was intermittent, the log showed it every time it happened.

## Lies, Damn Lies, and Statistics

The second reason to make it fail is to get a clue about the cause. When a problem is intermittent, you may start to see patterns in your actions that seem to be associated with the failure. This is okay, but don't get too carried away by it.

When failures are random, you probably can't take enough statistical samples to know whether clicking that button with your left hand instead of your right makes as big a difference as it seems to. A lot of times, coincidences will make you think that one condition makes the problem more likely to happen than some other condition. Then you start chasing "what's the difference between those two conditions?" and waste a lot of time barking up the wrong tree.

This doesn't mean that those coincidental differences you're seeing aren't, in fact, connected to the bug in some way. But if they don't have a *direct* effect, the connection will be hidden by other random factors, and your chances of figuring it out by looking at those differences are pretty slim. You'd do better betting the slots in Vegas.

When you capture enough information, as described in the previous section, you can identify things that are *always* associated with the bug or *never* associated with the bug. Those are the things to look at as you focus on likely causes of the problem.

## Did You Fix It, or Did You Get Lucky?

Randomness makes proving that you fixed it a lot harder, of course. If it failed one out of ten times in the test, and you "fix" it, and now it fails one out of thirty times but you give up testing after twenty-eight tries, you think you fixed it, but you didn't.

If you use statistical testing, the more samples you run, the better off you are. But it's far better to find a sequence of events that always goes with the failure—even if the sequence itself is intermittent, when it happens, you get 100 percent failure. Then when you think you've fixed the problem, run tests until the sequence occurs; if the sequence occurs but the failure doesn't, you've fixed the bug. You don't give up after twenty-eight tries, because you haven't seen the sequence yet. (You *may* give up after twenty-eight tries because the pizza has arrived, but then you'll have to go back to work after dinner—yet another reason for automated testing.)

**War Story.** We had an intermittent problem involving video calls using six phone lines at once. Videoconferencing systems need lots of bits per second to move video around, and one phone line is not enough. So the system makes six phone calls and distributes the video data over the six phone lines.

The trouble is, the phone company may not route all six calls via the same path, so the data on some calls may arrive a little later than the data on the other calls. To fix this, we use a method called *bonding*, in which the sending system puts marker information in each data stream that allows the other side to figure out what the various delays are. The other side then adds its own delay to the fast calls until they're all lined up again (see Figure 4-2).

Sometimes our systems would get garbled data as often as one out of five

Figure 4-2. Bonding with the Phone Network.

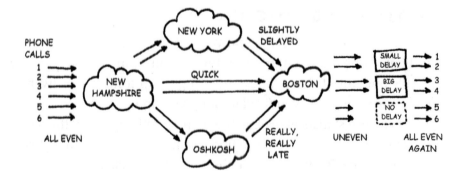

calls. At other times they could go sixty calls without a failure. Since bonding problems would cause this sort of garbled data, we added instrumentation to the systems to print out information about the six calls. What we found was that most of the time, the phone company connected the six calls in normal order, i.e., 1, 2, 3, 4, 5, and then 6. But on the calls that failed, the order was not normal, e.g., 1, 3, 2, 4, 5, 6.

This gave us the clue we needed to home in on the problem (handling out-of-sequence calls), and with further instrumentation we found the bug. When we fixed it, we ran a bunch of tests, but we didn't care that it worked when the instrumentation showed the normal call sequence. When the sequence came up out of order and the call still worked, we knew we had fixed it. ■

The funny sequence was dependent on phone company traffic and could come and go depending on the time of day and the calling habits of the teenagers living in the surrounding town. Testing the fix by waiting for the failure could have misled us if phone traffic was quiet at the time. But once we were able to associate the call sequence with the failure, we were no longer at the mercy of the local teenagers.

## "But That Can't Happen"

If you've worked with engineers for any appreciable time, you've heard this statement. A test person or field tech reports a problem, and the engineer cocks his head, puzzles for a moment, and says, "But that can't happen."

Sometimes the engineer is right—the tester messed up. But usually the tester didn't mess up, and the problem is real. However, in many of those cases, the engineer is still sort of right—"that" *can't* happen.

The key word here is "that." What is "that"? "That" is the failure mechanism that the tester or the engineer (or both) is *assuming* is behind the problem. Or "that" is the sequence of events that *seems to be* the key to reproducing the problem. And, in fact, it's possible that *that* "that" *can't* happen.

But the failure *did* happen. What test sequence triggered it and what bug caused it are still unclear. The next step is to forget about the assumptions and make it fail in the presence of the engineer. This proves that the test sequence was reported correctly, and it gives the engineer a chance to either eat his words about the impossibility of the failure or try a new test strategy that points to where the real, and entirely possible, failure is hiding.

Click and Clack of the *Car Talk* radio show posed an interesting puzzler. An owner complained that his 1976 Volare had trouble starting whenever he and his family went out for a certain flavor of ice cream. They often went to a local ice cream parlor and bought either vanilla, chocolate, or three-bean tofu mint chipped-beef. If they bought vanilla or chocolate, the car started up just fine. If they bought three-bean tofu mint chipped-beef, it would not start right up, but would crank and crank, eventually starting but running terribly.

The answer to the puzzler was that vanilla and chocolate ice cream, being popular, are prepacked in quart containers and ready to go. But hardly anyone buys three-bean tofu mint chipped-beef, so that has to be hand packed. And hand packing takes time—enough time for an old, carbureted Volare engine, sitting in the early evening summer heat, to suffer from vapor lock.* ▪

Now, you might be *absolutely positive* that the ice cream flavor could not affect the car. And you'd be right—*that* can't happen. But *buying* an odd flavor of ice cream *could* affect the car, and only by

---

*From the *Car Talk* section of cars.com, included by permission.

accepting the data and looking further into the situation can you discover *that* "that."

## Never Throw Away a Debugging Tool

Sometimes a test tool can be reused in other debugging situations. Think about this when you design it, and make it maintainable and upgradeable. This means using good engineering techniques, documentation, etc. Enter it into the source code control system. Build it into your systems so that it's always available in the field. Don't just code it like the throwaway tool you're thinking it is—you may be wrong about throwing it away.

Sometimes a tool is so useful you can actually sell it; many a company has changed its business after discovering that the tool it has developed is even more desirable than its products. A tool can be useful in ways that you never would have imagined, as in this follow-on to the TV game story:

**War Story.** I had forgotten about my automatic TV game paddle when, months later, we were proudly showing off our prototype to the entrepreneur who was funding the project. (Yes, he was the investor, and, amazingly enough, it didn't fail.) He liked the way it played, but he wasn't happy. He complained that there was no way to turn on two practice walls. (He'd seen an early prototype where unplugging both paddle controllers resulted in two practice walls, with the ball bouncing around between them.)

We were dumbfounded. Why would anyone want two practice walls? I mean, you have to have at least *one* paddle to actually practice, right? He said, "Oh, spoken like a true engineer. What you're missing is that I need something to help *sell* the game. I want this thing to be displayed in the stores and attract people by looking like someone's playing a game, even though no one is. The ball has to be bouncing around, and if you had two walls, it would do that."

You know where this is going, and so did I at the time, but no one else in the room did. Barely able to conceal my excitement, I calmly said, "Well, I have an idea that might work. Let me try it out." I calmly scooped up the circuit board and left the room. Once the door was safely closed, I uncalmly danced down the hall with glee. I added the debug circuit as quickly as I could (along with a switch for maximum dramatic effect), and within about four minutes I was back in the room again, outwardly very cool as I set the prototype in the middle of the conference room table. I got it playing with the manual paddle and the practice wall, and then flipped the switch. As the robotic paddle eerily followed the ball up and down, playing the game better than anyone had ever seen, not only were the eyes of our investor popping out of his head, but so were the eyes of my fellow engineers popping out of *theirs*. It was one of the high points of my fledgling career.

The game shipped with both a practice wall and a "practice paddle" option, and the stores displayed the game with both running. It sold very well. ▪

# Remember

### Make It Fail

It seems easy, but if you don't do it, debugging is hard.

- **Do it again.** Do it again so you can look at it, so you can focus on the cause, and so you can tell if you fixed it.

- **Start at the beginning.** The mechanic needs to know that the car went through the car wash before the windows froze.

- **Stimulate the failure.** Spray a hose on that leaky window.

- **But don't simulate the failure.** Spray a hose on the *leaky* window, not on a different, "similar" one.

- **Find the uncontrolled condition that makes it intermittent.** Vary everything you can—shake it, rattle it, roll it, and twist it until it shouts.

- **Record everything and find the signature of intermittent bugs.** Our bonding system always and only failed on jumbled calls.

- **Don't trust statistics too much.** The bonding problem seemed to be related to the time of day, but it was actually the local teenagers tying up the phone lines.

- **Know that "that"** *can* **happen.** Even the ice cream flavor can matter.

- **Never throw away a debugging tool.** A robot paddle might come in handy someday.

# 5

# Quit Thinking and Look

"It is a capital mistake to theorize before one has data. Insensibly one begins to twist facts to suit theories, instead of theories to suit facts."

—SHERLOCK HOLMES, *A SCANDAL IN BOHEMIA*

**War Story.** Our company built a circuit board that plugged into a personal computer and included its own slave microprocessor, with its own memory (see Figure 5-1). Before the host (main) computer could start up the slave microprocessor, it had to download the slave's program memory; this was accomplished with a special mechanism in the slave, which allowed data to be sent from the host through the slave to the memory. When this was done, the slave would check for errors in the contents of the memory (using a magical thing called a checksum). If the memory was okay, the slave would start running. If it wasn't okay, the slave

Figure 5-1. The Corrupt System.

would complain to the host and, given that its program was corrupt, would not try to run. (Obviously, this microprocessor would not go far in politics.)

The problem was that occasionally the slave would report an error and stop after the download. It was intermittent, happening maybe one in ten times and only in some of the systems. And, of course, it needed only one bad byte out of the 65,000 downloaded to cause the error. A couple of junior hardware guys were assigned to find and fix the problem.

They first wrote a test program in which the host wrote data across the host bus into one of the slave micro's registers, and then read it back again. They ran this "loopback" test millions of times, and the data they wrote always came back correct. So they said, "Well, we've tested it from the personal computer host bus down and into the slave micro, and that works fine, so the problem must be between the slave micro and the memory." They looked at the memory interface (trying to understand the circuit, which is a good thing, of course) and found that the timing was barely acceptable. "Gee," they said, "maybe there isn't quite enough hold time on the address for the memory even though it was supposed to be a glueless interface." (Junior engineers really do talk like that—except they use stronger words than gee.)

They decided to fix the timing and proceeded to design a small circuit board that would plug into the socket of the microprocessor. The board would contain the original micro along with some circuitry between the micro and the memory (see Figure 5-2). This design-and-build project took a long time; they were using a hand-wired prototype board, it was a complex chip, and there were wiring

**Figure 5-2. The Junior Engineers' Solution.**

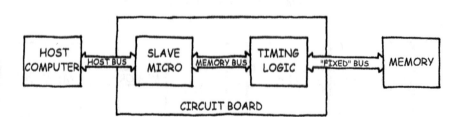

errors. They eventually managed to get the thing plugged in and working so they could finally, after several months, see whether this would solve the problem. It didn't. The memory still occasionally failed the checksum test.

Our senior engineer had been fairly uneasy about this whole approach to begin with, since no one had yet seen what was actually going wrong. Now he insisted that we see the bad data going into the memory. He got onto the job, broke out the heavy-duty logic analyzer, painstakingly hooked it up, and tried to figure out why the data was bad. He didn't really see any bad signals going in, but it was tough to figure out whether the data was right, because it was program data and looked random anyway. So he wrote a test that put a known, regular pattern of data in, a repeating loop of "00 55 AA FF." He expected to see errors in the data, like "00 54 AA FF," but what he actually saw was "00 55 55 AA FF." It wasn't that the wrong data was being written in, but that the right data was being written in twice.

He went back to the host bus side, put a scope on a few signals, and found that there was noise on the write line; because of other circuitry on the board, it had a small glitch in the middle that was occasionally big enough to make the pulse look like two pulses (see Figure 5-3).

When you write a register and read it back, as in the junior engineers' original test, using two write pulses just writes it twice; it still reads back correctly. But

## Figure 5-3. What the Senior Engineer Saw.

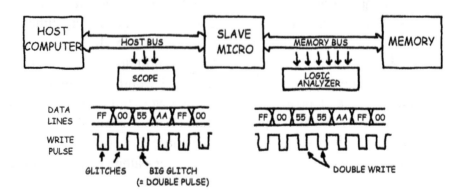

when you're downloading data through the chip, where each write sends another byte of data to the next location in memory, using two write pulses means that the second write goes to the next location and everything after that is off by one address. And you get a checksum error. We lost several months chasing the wrong thing because we guessed at the failure instead of looking at it. ▧

Actually seeing the low-level failure is crucial. If you guess at how something is failing, you often fix something that isn't the bug. Not only does the fix not work, but it takes time and money and may even break something else. Don't do it.

"Quit thinking and look." I make this statement to engineers more often than any other piece of debugging advice. We sometimes tease engineers who come up with an idea that seems pretty good on the surface, but on further examination isn't very good at all, by saying, "Well, he's a thinker." All engineers are thinkers. Engineers like to think. It's a fun thing to do, and it sure beats physical labor; that's why we became engineers in the first place. And while we think up all sorts of nifty things, there are more ways for something to be broken than even the most imaginative engineer can imagine. So why do we imagine we can find the problem by thinking about it? Because we're engineers, and thinking is *easier* than looking.

Looking is hard. Like the senior engineer in the example, you have to hook up a scope and a logic analyzer, which is very difficult, especially with chips so dense that you can't just clip on a probe. You've got to solder wires onto tiny pins, program logic analyzers, and figure out complex triggers. (In fact, I wondered whether this example was too long to open this chapter with, but I used it anyway because it helps make the point. Looking is often, if not always, more complicated than we would like.) In the software world, looking means putting in breakpoints, adding debug statements, monitoring program values, and examining memory. In the medical world, you run blood tests and take x-rays. It's a lot of work.

The shortcut, especially given Rule 1, "Understand the System," is to just try to figure it out:

> "Well, it must be the rammafram because it only fails when I turn on the frobnivator."

> "I ran a simulation and that worked fine, so the problem can't be there."

> And in the memory problem, "The timing is marginal. We'd better redesign the whole circuit. That will fix it."

Those are all very easy (and popular!) statements to make (well, maybe not the frobnivator statement), and seem to offer easier ways to find the problem, except that they usually don't.

I once worked with a guy who was pretty sharp and took great pride in both his ability to think logically and his understanding of our products. When he heard about a bug, he would regularly say, "I bet it's a such-and-such problem." I always told him I would take the bet. We never put money on it, and it's too bad—I would have won almost every time. He was smart and he understood the system, but he didn't look at the failure and therefore didn't have nearly enough information to figure it out.

When you're all done disproving your bad guesses, you still have to find the bug. You still have the same amount of work to do that you had before, only now you have less time. This is bad, unless you're one of those people who believe that the sooner you fall behind, the more time you have to catch up. So here are some guidelines to help you look before you think.

## See the Failure

It seems obvious that if you want to find a failure, you have to actually see the failure occur. In fact, if you don't see the failure, you won't even know it happened, right? Not true. What we see when we note the bug is the *result* of the failure: I turned on the switch and the light didn't come on. But what was the actual failure? Was it that the electricity couldn't get through the broken switch, or that it couldn't get through the broken bulb filament? (Or did I flip the wrong switch?) You have to look closely to see the failure in enough detail to debug it. In the slave micro story, the junior engineers didn't look at the memory being written incorrectly as a result of bad timing. And had they looked, they wouldn't have seen it, because it wasn't happening.

Many problems are easily misinterpreted if you can't see all the way to what's actually happening. You end up fixing something that you've guessed is the problem, but in fact it was something completely different that failed. Because you didn't actually see a bit change, a subroutine get called with the wrong parameter, or a queue overrun, you go and fix something that didn't actually break. Not only haven't you fixed the problem, but you might actually change the timing so it hides the problem and makes you think you fixed it. Even worse, you may break something else. At best, it costs you money and time, like the guy who buys a new set of golf clubs instead of having a golf pro analyze his swing. New clubs aren't going to help his slice, the golf lesson is cheaper, and he'll hit a lot of double-bogey rounds until he finally relents and takes the lesson.

**War Story.** My boss did a favor for a neighbor who happened to sell pumps for a living. The neighbor felt that he owed a return favor and promised, "If you ever need a new well pump, I'll take care of it, and I'll set you up with the best pump there is." One week, while my boss was away on business, his wife heard a motor run for ten seconds or so, then stop. It happened only occasionally, every few hours. Since her husband was away, she called the neighbor to see what he thought. "It's the well pump!" he responded, and he proceeded to take care of the problem the next day. His crew came over, pulled the old pump, installed the new one, and left, having done a good job and having returned a favor. Except that messing with the pump stirred up the sediment in the well so that they had to deal with murky water and chlorine for a few days. Oh, and also the motor sound kept on happening.

That evening, when my boss spoke to his wife on the phone, he found out about this turn of events. "What made you think it was the pump? Was there any loss of water pressure?" "No." "Any puddles on the basement floor?" "No." "Did anyone actually stand near the pump when it made the noise?" "No."

It turned out that before he left, my boss had decided to put some air into his tires and had used an electric compressor in the garage. When he left, he left the compressor on, and as air leaked out of the hose, every now and then the motor would kick in to bring the pressure back up. The old water pump was fine; while replacing it didn't actually cost my boss any money, he did have to deal with the subsequent sediment and chlorine. And I imagine his wife and his neighbor had to deal with the subsequent comments about their debugging techniques. ■

**War Story.** An associate of mine told me about a problem his company had with a server computer that apparently crashed and restarted late every evening, at about the same time. They had logs of the restart, but nothing that indicated what had caused the problem. They tried to monitor processes that were running automatically, figuring that since the server failed at about the same time every evening, the problem must be something automatic. But after a few weeks of this, nothing seemed to correlate. So my friend decided to stay at work late and just watch the machine. At a little after 11 P.M., the machine's power suddenly went off. My friend looked behind him and found the janitor, who had just unplugged the server to "borrow" the outlet for his vacuum cleaner. The janitor figured it was okay, since he'd been doing it every night for weeks. The problem was obvious once someone actually looked at it while it failed. ▦

Make sure you see what's actually going wrong. Looking is usually much quicker than the guesswork shortcut, because the shortcut often leads nowhere.

## See the Details

The examples just given are extreme—the amount of looking required was minimal (although the protagonists didn't even do that at first). More typically, each time you look into the system to see the failure, you learn more about what's failing. This will help you decide where to look even deeper to get more detail. Eventually, you get enough detail that it makes sense to look at the design and figure out what the cause of the problem is.

**War Story.** We were working on video compression software, which transmits video from one place to another using very few bits. If it's working right, you get pretty good video out; if it's not, the picture looks blocky and strange. Ours was looking more blocky and strange than we intended, so we figured something was wrong somewhere.

Now, video compression uses many techniques to save bits; rather than just sending all the pixels (dots) in each frame (at thirty frames per second), it tries to eliminate redundant information. For example, if the background hasn't changed, it sends a "no change" bit and the other side just redisplays the background from the previous frame. There are dozens of different, interrelated mechanisms like this, all affecting the video quality and all very difficult to analyze and correct.

Without a better idea of what was really happening, we could have guessed and coded for months in our efforts to improve the video.

One compression technique, called motion estimation, searches to see if a part of a picture (like my hand) has moved to a new place in the next frame (like when I wave). (Video compression engineers do a *lot* of hand waving.) If it can find motion, it can represent the new picture in a few bits, essentially saying, "This part of the picture is just the previous picture moved X pixels over and Y pixels up" (see Figure 5-4). It doesn't have to say what the part looks like; as in the background case, the other side already knows that from the previous picture. If it can't find motion, it has to describe the hand all over again, which takes lots of bits and produces a low-quality picture.

**Figure 5-4. Motion Estimation.**

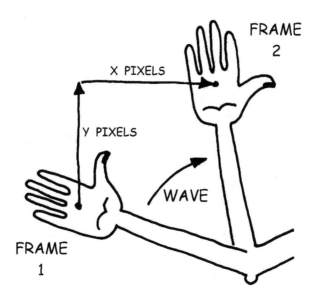

The moving objects looked the worst, so we decided to take a deeper look at the motion estimation. But we didn't try to optimize yet, or even to analyze the code. We just wanted to see if the system was finding the moving objects. So we added some software that would show detected motion as little squares right on the output screen, coded by color for direction and by brightness for magnitude. Now when I moved my hand downward, I saw it covered with orange boxes, and the faster I moved it, the brighter the boxes were. When I moved my hand upward, I saw purple. When I waved it left or right, I saw green and blue boxes, *but there weren't nearly as many.*

Wondering why the system wasn't detecting left-right motion as well, we output detailed snapshots of the motion calculations onto a separate debug monitor, including information about how well the picture matched at any search location. We were surprised to see that the software was searching only a few horizontal locations and skipping the rest. The match algorithm wasn't broken; the reason it was missing matches was that the search algorithm wasn't looking in all the possible places. We fixed the simple bug in the search code and got lots of horizontal motion detection, as well as a much better picture. ▪

How deep should you go before you stop looking and start thinking again? The simple answer is, "Keep looking until the failure you can see has a limited number of possible causes to examine." In the previous example, once we saw that the search was incomplete, we looked at the search code and found the bug. The visible failure was that the search never got to all the locations. Should we have then stepped through the code to watch it fail? Probably not—the search was controlled by one small, simple software routine. Should we have looked at the code earlier, after we saw that we weren't detecting horizontal motion? Absolutely not—there are lots of ways the search could fail, even if it looked at every position. We would have wasted time examining the code that decides whether the picture matches, instead of concentrating on where it searches. So we didn't stop there; we went deep enough to see that the problem was a search failure and not a match failure.

In the well pump example, they started fixing the problem without even going into the basement to listen. If they had, they'd have heard that the sound was coming from the compressor in the garage, rather than from the pump in the well. They made their guess while there were still too many machines that could possibly be at fault.

Experience helps here, as does understanding your system. As you make and chase bad guesses, you'll get a feel for how deep you have to see in a given case. You'll know when the failure you see implicates a small enough piece of the design. And you'll understand that the measure of a good debugger is not how soon you come up with a guess or how good your guesses are, but how few bad guesses you actually act on.

## Now You See It, Now You Don't

Seeing the failure in low-level detail has another advantage in dealing with intermittent bugs, which we've discussed before and will discuss again: Once you have this view of the failure, when you think you've fixed the bug, it's easy to prove that you did fix the bug. You don't have to rely on statistics; you can *see* that the error doesn't happen anymore. When our senior engineer fixed the noise problem on our slave microprocessor, he could see that the glitch in the write pulse was gone.

## Instrument the System

Now that you've decided to open your eyes, the next thing you need to do is shed some light on the subject. You have to put instrumentation into or onto the system. Into the system is best; during design, build in tools that will help you see what's going on inside. What the heck, you're building in the bugs at that point; you might as well build in the debugging tools as well. But since you can't predict at design time everything you'll need to see at debug time, you'll miss things, and you'll have to either build special versions of the system just to include the instrumentation or add on external instrumentation.

## Design Instrumentation In

In the world of electronic hardware, this means test points, test points, and more test points. Add a test connector to allow easy access to buses and important signals. These days, with programmable gate arrays and application-specific integrated circuits, the problem is often buried inside a chunk of logic that you can't get into with external instruments, so the more signals you can bring out of the chip, the better off you'll be. Make all registers readable as well as writable. Add LEDs and status displays to help you see what's going on in the circuit. Have you noticed that some personal computers can tell you the temperature of the main processor when you run the system status software? That's because the designers built the temperature sensor in—since the processor is usually all closed up inside the case, that's the only way to tell when it gets too hot.

In the software world, the first level of built-in instrumentation is usually compiling in debug mode so you can watch your program run with a source code debugger. Unfortunately, when it's time to ship that program, you have to compile in release mode, so the source debugger is not an option for debugging product code. So you turn to your next option (no, not quitting the business and becoming a rock star), which is to put interesting variables into performance monitors so you can watch them during run time. In any case, implement a debug window and have your code spit out status messages. Of course, make the window capable of saving the messages into a debug log file.

The more status messages you get, the better, but you should have some way to switch selected messages or types of messages on and off, so you can focus on the ones you need in order to debug a particular problem. Also, spewing messages to a debug window often changes timing, which can affect the bug. (A common lament is that turning on the debugger slows the system enough to make it stop failing—"That's why they call it a debugger." See "The Heisenberg Uncertainty Principle" a little further on.) Sending too many messages to a window may also bring the system processor to its knees; when every mouse click takes thirty-five seconds, you tend to get annoyed.

Status messages can be switched on and off at three different levels: compile time, start-up time, and run time. Switching at compile time saves code, but it prevents debugging after you've released the product. Switching at start-up time is easy to implement, but it means that you can't debug a problem once the system is running. Switching at run time is harder to code but allows the ultimate flexibility—you can debug at any time. If you use start-up or run-time switches, you can even tell a customer how to turn status messages on and debug remotely. (This is a good reason to make sure your debug statements are spelled right and contain no obscene, politically incorrect, or cynical antimanagement content.)

The format of your status messages can make a big difference in later analysis. Break the messages into fields, so that certain information always appears in a particular column. One column should be a system time stamp that's accurate enough to deal with timing problems. There are many other candidates for standard columns: the module or source file that outputs the message; a general code for message type, such as "info," "error," or "really nasty error"; the initials of the engineer who wrote the output message, to help track down who worked on what and why they can't spell; and run-time data such as commands, status codes, and expected versus actual values to give you the real details you'll need later. Finally, by using consistent formats and keywords, you can filter the debug logs afterward to help you focus on the stuff you need to see.

In embedded systems (where the computer has no display, keyboard, or mouse), software instrumentation means adding some sort of output display: a serial port or a liquid crystal display panel. Most DSPs have development ports for monitoring the real-time operating system from a separate PC. If the embedded processor is built into another computer, use the main processor's display; add communication such as shared memory locations or message registers between the embedded processor and the main computer. For looking at code timing problems without a real-time operating system, add a couple of hardware bits that you can toggle up and down when you get into and out of routines; you can look at these bits with a hardware scope. An in-circuit emulator gives you a way to trace through all the silly and mischievous things your code does when it thinks no one is watching.

Be careful with in-circuit emulators, though—while they're a great tool for debugging software, they're notoriously not the same as the hardware processor you normally plug in. Not only are there timing and memory mapping differences, but sometimes entire functions are removed. As a result, emulators can't be used to verify the *hardware* design of an embedded processor circuit. However, once you've designed a circuit that can handle the eccentricities of the emulator, it's a marvelous way to instrument embedded circuit *software.*

The bottom line here is that you should think about debugging right from the start of the design process. Make sure that instrumentation is part of the product requirements. Make sure that hooks for instrumentation are part of every functional spec and API definition.

Make the debug monitor and analysis filter part of your standard utility set. And there's a bonus: Besides making the eventual debugging process easier, thinking about what needs instrumentation helps you design the system better and avoid some of the bugs in the first place.

### Build Instrumentation In Later

No matter how much thinking you do during design, when you start debugging, you're going to have to look at something you didn't anticipate. This is okay; you just have to build in the instrumentation when you need it. But there are some caveats.

Be careful to start with the same design base that the bug was found in (so you don't simulate the failure) and add what you need. This means the same build of software and/or the same revision of hardware. Once you get the instrumentation in, make it fail again to prove that you *did* use the right base, and that your instrumentation didn't affect the problem. (See the Heisenberg section a little later.) Finally, once you've found the problem, take all that stuff out so it doesn't clutter up the resulting product. (Of course, you should always keep a copy around in case you need it later—comment or "#ifdef" it out instead of deleting it.)

The nice thing about ad hoc instrumentation is that it can show you whatever you need to see:

**War Story.** I had a programmable gate array once that was acting strange, so I recompiled it to use a couple of spare external pins as scope probes into the system. I had to recompile the array every time I wanted to look at a new signal, but I was able to see what I needed and solve the problem. ■

Raw data from a program is often in a form that isn't convenient to analyze. No problem; your ad hoc instrumentation can massage the data to make the details you need more obvious:

**War Story.** We had a communications system that was corrupting the data as it traveled through several buffer stages. We didn't know whether data was getting overwritten or dropped, so we added debug statements that output the values of the pointers for the memory buffers. The pointers were large hex numbers, and it was really the size of the space between them that we were worried about, so we added a calculation to determine the difference between the pointers (including the wraparound at the end of the buffer) and output that, too. It was then easy to see that the read pointer was occasionally getting bumped up an extra time, which eventually caused data to be read out ahead of where it was being written. We analyzed the small part of the code that touched the pointer and quickly found the bug. ▧

What should you look for? Look for things that will either confirm what you expect or show you the unexpected behavior that's causing the bug. In the next chapter, "Divide and Conquer," you'll get some more detailed search strategy tips, but at this level, the key is to get pertinent details. Look at variables, pointers, buffer levels, memory allocation, event timing relationships, semaphore flags, and error flags. Look at function calls and exits, along with their parameters and return values. Look at commands, data, window messages, and network packets. *Get the details.* In the motion estimation story, we found the bad search algorithm by outputting the search locations and match scores.

## Don't Be Afraid to Dive In

I've seen advice on debugging production (i.e., released) software that says, "Since you can't modify the software and it has no source debugging capability, you should use the existing APIs and swap modules in and out to isolate the failing module." I hate this advice. It violates the "don't simulate the failure" rule; presupposes that your APIs and modules are conveniently architected; and, even if you do isolate the problem to a module, leaves you with no way of looking any deeper, so that you have to think and not look. Ugh.

If there's a bug in the code, you're going to have to rebuild the software in order to fix it. Therefore, you should be willing to rebuild the software in order to find the bug in the first place. Make a debug version so you can see the source. Add new debug statements to look at the parameters you really need to see. "Quit Thinking and Look," and then, when you've fixed the bug, "#ifdef" all that stuff out and ship production code again.

Earlier, I mentioned sending an engineer to the customer site with a taxi-load of instrumentation. Because customer sites are usually production code and it's difficult to build software offsite, field engineers usually have to use add-on or already built-in instrumentation. But when that isn't enough, you'll want to create a simulation in your own lab so you can add tests to the software. Of course, you need to make sure that it actually fails in the lab in order to be sure that you got away with your simulation. If it doesn't fail in the lab, you'll have to add instrumentation to the software in the field; send the engineers to Aruba with a laptop and a modem; then build what they need in the lab and e-mail it to them.

## Add Instrumentation On

If you didn't or couldn't build instrumentation in, at the very least, add it on. In hardware, use meters, scopes, logic analyzers, spectrum analyzers, thermocouples, or whatever else you need to see your hardware. You'll need extender boards if you're working inside a PC. Also, all your equipment has to be fast enough and accurate enough to measure the sorts of things you're looking for. A low-frequency scope isn't going to help you find high-frequency problems, and a digital logic analyzer isn't going to help you see noise and glitches. Your finger may tell you that a chip is too hot to touch (and that you were foolish to touch it), but it won't tell you if the chip is too hot to run properly.

For software, if you can't use a debugger to get an inside view of your code, sometimes you can hook up a bus-oriented analyzer that can disassemble the instructions as they go by. Because you get only assembly language debugging, however, this is a last resort, unless you're one of those "wooden ships and iron men" diehards who waxes nostalgic over assembly language. (The warning signs: You know the ASCII code, you can add and subtract in hexadecimal, and you really care about the state of the carry bit.)

**War Story.** We once used a VCR as an external instrument to debug a video display problem. It looked as if the system was displaying frames out of order, but we recorded the video and then used the frame-by-frame stepping feature of the VCR to show that the system was actually displaying the same frame twice, and that the interlace of the TV made that seem like the video actually went backward. ▪

## Instrumentation in Daily Life

In the medical world, we take temperatures with a thermometer and look for cancer with x-rays. Electrocardiography machines (which measure electrical signals in the heart) have a probe pod that looks exactly like a logic analyzer pod; they might have used the same plastic case. We have to use these external instruments, because it's too late in the design cycle to build internal instrumentation into the human body. But part of modern medical science is discovering what instrumentation is already built in. Examples of this are marker genes for hereditary diseases or the presence of chemicals that indicate prostate cancer. (In that case, using the built-in instrumentation is a lot more pleasant than the alternative digital probe!)

Plumbers build instrumentation into the system when they add a temperature gauge to a boiler or a pressure gauge to a water tank. (In the well pump story, if they had checked the well pressure gauge, they would have seen that the pump was just fine. The air compressor had a gauge, too, which was undoubtedly drifting down slowly, and then up quickly when the compressor ran.)

To find air leaks in a house, we dangle a ribbon around the window frames and electrical outlets and look for drafts; if we can afford it, we might use an infrared sensor to look for cool spots. When you have a leak in a bicycle tire, you swab soapy water on it and look for the bubbles. (This is assuming that you can't just look for the huge nail in the tire, a form of built-in instrumentation.) You use soap bubbles to look for leaks around the gas tank of the backyard grill; you don't want to use the built-in instrumentation (a fiery explosion)—there's too much at steak. (Sorry.) Natural gas has a rotten egg odor *added to it* for the sole purpose of making it detectable when it's leaking. Scanning a beach with a metal detector sure beats digging randomly to find those old pennies and hair clips.

> "Only the spoon knows what is stirring in the pot."
>
> —SICILIAN PROVERB

## The Heisenberg Uncertainty Principle

Heisenberg was one of the pioneers of quantum physics. He was working with *really light, really tiny* atomic particles, and he realized that you can measure either where a particle is or where it's going, but the more precisely you measure one of these aspects, the more you disturb the other. You just can't get an accurate measurement, because your probes are part of the system. Which is to say, your test instrumentation affects the system under test.

The effect that a debugger has on timing was mentioned earlier. Any instrumentation can affect the system, to varying degrees. A scope probe adds capacitance to the circuit. Debug software versions affect timing and code size. Adding an extender card to a PCI bus changes the bus timing. Even opening the cover of a PC changes the temperature of the parts inside.

This is unavoidable. (I'm certain of it.) You just have to keep it in mind so the effects don't take you by surprise. Also, some instrumentation methods are less intrusive than others. Finding minerals with sonar is nicer to the environment than digging up a few square miles of coal country. An x-ray or a CAT scan is less intrusive than exploratory surgery—but may not be enough.

As mentioned in "Make It Fail," even minor changes can affect the system enough to hide the bug completely. Instrumentation is one of those changes, so after you've added instrumentation to a failing system, make it fail again to prove that Heisenberg isn't biting you.

## Guess Only to Focus the Search

"Quit Thinking and Look" doesn't mean that you don't ever make any guesses about what might be wrong. Guessing is a pretty good thing, especially if you understand the system. Your guesses may even be pretty close, but you should guess *only to focus the search*. You still have to confirm that your guess is correct by seeing the failure before you go about trying to fix the failure. In the video compression and motion estimation story, we *guessed* that motion estimation might not be working right, and therefore we started *looking* into the motion detection. We confirmed the guess when we waved left and right and *saw* just a few blue and green blocks. Then we *guessed* that the matching logic wasn't working and *looked* at the calculations; our guess was disproved when we *saw* that the search algorithm was broken.

So don't trust your guesses too much; often they're way off and will lead you down the wrong path. If it turns out that careful instrumentation doesn't confirm a particular guess, then it's time to back up and guess again. (Or reconsult your Ouija board, or throw another dart at your "bug cause" dartboard—whatever your methodology may be. I recommend the use of Rule 4: "Divide and Conquer.") Our senior engineer in the slave microprocessor story first looked for garbled data going into the memory, but he didn't find it. Then he found repeated data and refocused his search on the host side of the microprocessor, which is where he found the double write pulse.

An exception: One reason for guessing in a particular way is that some problems are more likely than others or easier to fix than others, so you check those out first. In fact, when you make a particular guess because that problem is *both* very likely *and* easy to fix, that's the one time you should try a fix without actually seeing the details of the failure. In an earlier example I mentioned turning on a switch and a light not coming on, and I suggested that the problem could be either a bad switch or a bad bulb. But it's far more likely to be a bad bulb, and that's easy to fix, so you just do it; if the new bulb works, you're done. But I bet that even then you shake the old bulb, just to be sure there's a broken filament rattling around inside.

**War Story.** A friend of mine has an in-sink hot water dispenser. It has an electric heater in it, and one day the water wasn't coming out hot. He called up the service line and was told that it might be the internal fuse. So he went out and bought a fuse (a strange-looking six-inch wire) and, working in cramped conditions, managed with difficulty to replace the old fuse. Still no hot water. The problem turned out to be the circuit breaker, which took a few seconds to reset, including opening the breaker panel and finding the right breaker. Not only had my friend guessed the wrong solution, but he had guessed the one that was difficult to implement. He never told me how much the fuse cost. ▦

# Remember

### Quit Thinking and Look

You can think up thousands of possible reasons for a failure. *You can see only the actual cause.*

- **See the failure.** The senior engineer *saw* the real failure and was able to find the cause. The junior guys *thought* they *knew* what the failure was and fixed something that wasn't broken.

- **See the details.** Don't stop when you hear the pump. Go down to the basement and find out *which* pump.

- **Build instrumentation in.** Use source code debuggers, debug logs, status messages, flashing lights, and rotten egg odors.

- **Add instrumentation on.** Use analyzers, scopes, meters, metal detectors, electrocardiography machines, and soap bubbles.

- **Don't be afraid to dive in.** So it's production software. It's broken, and you'll have to open it up to fix it.

- **Watch out for Heisenberg.** Don't let your instruments overwhelm your system.

- **Guess only to focus the search.** Go ahead and guess that the memory timing is bad, but look at it before you build a timing fixer.

chapter

6

# Divide and Conquer

"How often have I said to you that when you have eliminated the impossible, whatever remains, however improbable, must be the truth?"

—SHERLOCK HOLMES, *THE SIGN OF THE FOUR*

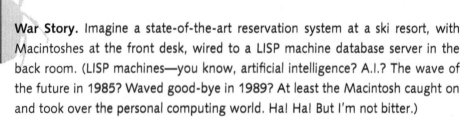

**War Story.** Imagine a state-of-the-art reservation system at a ski resort, with Macintoshes at the front desk, wired to a LISP machine database server in the back room. (LISP machines—you know, artificial intelligence? A.I.? The wave of the future in 1985? Waved good-bye in 1989? At least the Macintosh caught on and took over the personal computing world. Ha! Ha! But I'm not bitter.)

The resort staff complained that the Macintosh terminals were becoming slower and slower when they tried to get records from the database machine. One terminal was very slow (and seemed to have always been very slow) and sometimes failed to complete the database lookup, displaying an error message. A technician was dispatched, and in the middle of the night (it was a working hotel) he took a look at the problem. He understood the system: The database machine and the terminals communicated over serial lines and checked the information they transferred for errors. If there was an error, the computers would retry until they got it right, or report the error if they couldn't get it right for a long time. The technician guessed, correctly, that there were communication errors, which were causing the systems to take longer because they had to keep retrying the transmissions. He confirmed this by looking at debug messages in the communication software, which showed that there were errors and retries on data going in both directions. Since apparently no software had changed since the system had last worked okay, he guessed that the problem was in the hardware.

The hardware consisted of a special circuit board in the database machine that had eight communication circuits coming out of it on a single flat ribbon cable. The cable went to a "breakout box" mounted on the wall, which had eight serial line connectors on the front of it. The point of the breakout box was to make space for all the connectors; there was no room to put eight connectors into the back of the database machine. The eight serial cables from the breakout box went to the Macintosh terminals (see Figure 6-1).

The technician didn't know if the problem was the circuit board in the database computer or the wiring to the terminals, but since all the terminals were acting up, he assumed that it wasn't the terminals. Using an oscilloscope, he looked at the place where the circuit board and wiring meet—the computer end of the flat cable. (There were constant "Are you there?" messages between the terminals and the database machine, so he had signals to look at in both directions.) He discovered that strong, good signals were going out to the terminals and weak, bad signals were coming in.

**Figure 6-1. The Hotel Reservation System.**

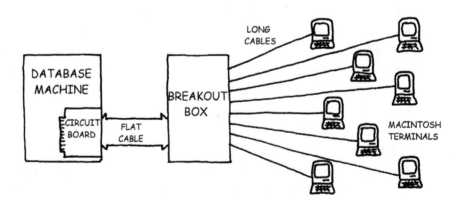

Relieved that the problem wasn't the complex and expensive circuit board, but surprised that it could be the usually reliable cabling, he went to an easily accessible point that was "halfway" along the wiring path to the terminals. He looked at the signals where the eight serial lines plugged into the breakout box. This time, the goodness was reversed: The good stuff was coming in from the terminals, and the bad stuff was going out. He knew from the debug messages that he had problems in both directions, and now he knew that the problems were between the two hardware points he'd looked at. So he split the difference again and looked at the flat cable where it was plugged into the breakout box— and again the goodness reversed, with good going out and bad coming in. The problem seemed to be in the breakout box. To prove this, he measured the resistance (unwillingness to let electric signals through) of the breakout box from the serial cable connector to the flat cable connector (i.e., between the last two points he'd tested) and found unreasonably high values. He then opened up the box.

There was nothing in the box but connectors soldered to a circuit board. Measuring the resistance at various points along the path, he discovered that there was high resistance where the serial connector pins were soldered to the circuit board. He looked closely at the connections and saw what looked like hairline cracks around each pin. He touched each pin with a hot soldering iron to remelt the solder and fix the connection. The resistance went back down nicely. After he did this with all the pins, he plugged in the lines and proved that the terminals worked. *Then* he unplugged everything, reassembled the box, plugged everything back in, and reconfirmed that the terminals worked. This was to accommodate Goldberg's Corollary to Murphy's Law, which states that *reassembling any more than is absolutely necessary before testing makes it probable that you have not fixed the problem and will have to disassemble everything again, with a probability that increases in proportion to the amount of reassembly effort involved.*

All the terminals worked, except for the really slow terminal. It was still very slow.

The technician got another cup of coffee and looked at new debug logs for the slow terminal. They now showed errors on the data going out to the terminal, but not on the data coming in. He opened up the serial cable connector where it plugged into the breakout box and looked at the signal again. The outgoing signal looked good. He moved "downstream" to the terminal, opened up the connector, looked at the signal coming in to the terminal, and found to his surprise that one of the wires wasn't even hooked up.

He looked at the wiring diagram, which showed that the cable had six wires in it, two for signals going in, two for signals going out, and two unconnected spares. (Since six-wire cable was the cheapest and easiest to get, it was better to waste wires than to buy four-wire cable.) The person who had wired the cable probably hadn't looked at the wiring diagram (or wired it in bad light, or was color-blind) and had hooked up the blue wire instead of the purple one—at one end. At the other end, the purple wire was correctly hooked up. Insidiously, the blue wire and the purple wire, which were not connected to each other but ran alongside each other through a hundred feet of cable, managed to couple enough signal between them to make the terminal work, although poorly. Once the technician hooked up the purple wire at both ends, the terminal worked perfectly. ▨

A number of debugging rules were put into play in this story. The technician "Understood the System" and used that information to focus the search on the hardware. He didn't just replace all the hardware, however, because he "Quit Thinking and Looked." (Certainly there was no way anyone would have guessed that the slow terminal wasn't even hooked up—anyone would expect that a wiring error like that would have stopped the terminal from *ever* working.) He used the built-in instrumentation to detect the communication errors and which direction they were in. He used the constant communication that was going on between the systems to "Make It Fail" regularly so he could see the problem with the scope. He saw the actual failure by measuring the resistance of the solder connections, and he verified that resoldering fixed the failure by measuring the resistance afterward. And when the wiring seemed kind of funny, he looked it up.

But the rule that our technician demonstrated particularly well with this debugging session was "Divide and Conquer." He narrowed the search by repeatedly splitting up the search space into a good half and a bad half, then looking further into the bad half for the problem.

First, he divided the system into software and hardware, and because he knew that the problem had been getting worse over time, he guessed that the problem was hardware. Then he looked at hardware signals halfway along the path; seeing bad signals confirmed his hardware guess. He continued to look at signals, and each time he saw badness on one side, he moved his search halfway along the path in the direction of the badness. When he went past the badness (it was now on the computer side), his next look was halfway back to his previous test point. Even when the breakout box was opened up, he worked his way along the path with a meter to locate precisely where the high-resistance connection was (see Figure 6-2).

## Narrow the Search

You may have noticed that "Divide and Conquer" is the first rule that actually involves finding the problem. In fact, it's the *only* rule that actually involves finding the problem. All of the others are just to help you follow this one. This rule is at the heart of debugging, and many people understand it naturally. Naturally, many people don't—hence this chapter.

Narrow the search. Home in on the problem. Find the range of the target. The common technique used in any efficient target search is called *successive approximation*—you want to find something within a range of possibilities, so you start at one end of the range,

Figure 6-2.  Follow the Numbered Steps.

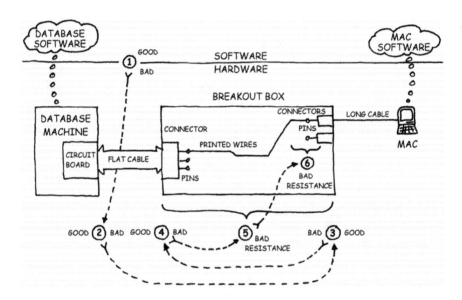

then go halfway to the other end and see if you're past it or not. If you're past it, you go to one-fourth and try again. If you're not past it, you go to three-fourths and try again. Each try, you figure out which direction the target is from where you are and move half the distance of the previous move toward the target. After a small number of attempts, you home right in on it.

Try to guess a number between 1 and 100, where a friend who knows the number tells you if each guess is too high or not; you can do it in seven guesses. If the answer is 42, your guesses might be 50, 25, 38, 44, 41, 43, and 42. If there are a hundred places where a bug might be, you want to find that bug in seven tries, not in a hundred, or fifty, or even twenty. Software search algorithms use this method for scanning large databases without taking forever. In hardware, high-speed analog-to-digital converters converge on the input voltage by testing output values, working from high-order to low-order bit. (Each bit is worth half of the previous bit—it's going halfway each time.) I imagine old-time ship cannoneers using successive approximation to home in on the target as quickly as possible; you really want to work fast when the trouble is shooting back at you.

**War Story.** I used to work summers for the phone company, on the "frame." This is where all the cables from the houses come into the building and are terminated on the "verticals," a line of a hundred or so posts with a few hundred numbered connections on each. Against the back of these posts are "horizontals," which are shelves with connections along the front edge that go to the central office switching equipment. To connect a house to a switch, you hook up a pair of wires from the vertical cable connection, run it down to the proper horizontal shelf, then run it along the shelf to the proper switch connection. Any cable connection can reach any switch connection. It's old-fashioned technology, but it works great.

Of course, the phone company has to keep track of which house is connected to which switch, and occasionally someone screws up and a wire isn't hooked up to the right place (sometimes you just can't hire good summer help). Now you've got this wire that you've disconnected from the vertical, and you want to find out where it's attached to the horizontal.

The first thing you do is look at which way the wire goes when it reaches the shelf. Then you hand the wire end to a helper, go around to the horizontal side, and go halfway to the end of the shelf in the direction the wire goes. You stick your hands and arms into the mass of wires running along the shelf (there are thousands) and feel for motion, while your helper yanks on the wire, stretching it and creating the motion. You can actually feel the stretching motion and find the wire pretty easily, amazingly enough; if you can't, the wire doesn't go that far, so you move halfway back toward the yanker. Once you feel the wire, you grab it and become the yanker; the helper becomes the feeler and moves halfway away again. After repeated leapfrogging, the two of you home in on the point where the wire is connected to the horizontal. This was standard procedure, except that if I had used the terms *yanker* and *feeler* I probably would have been hit with a union grievance. ■

Successive approximation depends on two very important details: You have to know the range of the search, and when you look at a point, you have to know which side of the problem you're on. If you do the 1 to 100 number-guessing game and your friend picks 135, or refuses to tell you whether or not you're too high, or lies and changes the answer each time, you will not succeed in guessing. (You should also find a new friend to play with.)

### In the Ballpark

Finding the range is easy if you assume that the entire system is the range. This can be a much bigger range than you'd like, but each guess cuts the range in half, so it's not a bad way to proceed. Our technician started with the whole system and used his first guess to cut the range to hardware, eliminating software from consideration. If he had guessed that the circuit board was the problem and limited his range to that, his search would have closed in on the edge of his range at the flat cable, and he would not have found the bug. Then he would have cursed, kicked himself for being so cocky, and widened his range again. In the number-guessing game, if your "friend" picks 135, you will quickly reach a guess of 100 and, finding that too low, pick a new range.

We'll talk more later about checking your assumptions, which is a way of widening your search range.

### Which Side Are You On?

Our hotel technician was actually quite lucky in his initial search, because the problem occurred in both directions of signal flow, but at the same place in the wiring. He was able to see bad signals no matter where he looked, and he simply moved in the direction the bad signals were coming from.

In the second part of the search, however, he had bad data only going out to the terminal; the data coming in from the terminal was fine. This is typical of most debugging situations: Things start out good, but somewhere along the way, they become bad. Data flows around a system and gets corrupted when it hits the bug. A program runs fine for a while and then crashes when it hits the bug. A windshield remains clean as you drive around and then gets splattered when it hits the bug.

You have to know your search range, and you have to know that at one end things are good and at the other, things are bad. Let's call this upstream (good, clear water) and downstream (bad, smelly, pink water). You're looking for the factory waste pipe that's dumping the smelly pink goo into the stream. Each time you look at a point, if everything is good, you assume that the problem is downstream of where you're looking. If the water is pink and smelly, you assume that the problem is upstream.

This is all very obvious when the problem is a smelly pink goo factory, but how does that relate to electronics or software? Generally, in hardware and data flow software, downstream means farther out in the signal or data flow. If the problem is a software crash, downstream means later in the code flow. (In this particular case, you put a breakpoint or message at a point. If the code gets there, the crash is farther along downstream. If it crashes before it gets to the breakpoint, the crash is upstream.) If a complex software calculation doesn't work, stop the process in the middle and see if the results so far are correct; if they're not, move upstream (earlier), and if they are, move downstream (later).

In my powder-weighing system (see Chapter 3), the interrupt was supposed to flow from the scale to the computer; upstream was the scale, downstream was the computer, and the bug was in the control chip in between. In the video compression example in Chapter 5, the motion estimator calculates a new location to search, and then tries to match the image; we saw that the system wasn't searching new locations correctly, so we ignored the downstream matching logic and looked upstream at the search logic.

## Inject Easy-to-Spot Patterns

It's pretty easy to see when clean water becomes pink and smelly, but what do you do when the effect of the bug is more subtle, or when the data is already so random looking that even a major corruption is invisible? One way to make a subtle effect more obvious is to use a really easy-to-recognize input or test pattern. In the stream example, normal data might be like a muddy stream—the goo is hard to spot. You have to eliminate the mud and use clean water. In the initial "Quit Thinking and Look" war story, I described how the senior engineer couldn't deal with random program data, so he injected "00 55 AA FF" into the stream and could easily see when it got clobbered. In the war story that begins the next chapter, you'll see how a test pattern, followed through a series of processing steps, helped find an audio bug.

In my work with video engines, I've often used a video pattern that smoothly changes color across the screen, so that mapping errors show up as lines or edges. You've seen this technique if you've ever changed the video resolution of your PC; when you hit the "test" button, it puts up a bunch of patterns and colors, all labeled so you know what they should look like. If they don't look right, that video mode won't work on your machine.

In the motion estimation story, we created a known input by waving—we knew where on the screen the motion was and what direction it was in. We could look at the calculation data knowing what to expect.

**War Story.** In the last chapter, I described a situation where we used a VCR to capture video output and look for out-of-sequence frames. We could tell whether the frames were out of sequence because we aimed the input camera at a wheel with alternating-color wedges (like a pizza on acid) that was turning at exactly one revolution every four seconds. We had markings around the outside that indicated one-thirtieth of a second, or one frame time. The wedges were supposed to move one mark every frame; if there was a frame out of order or a repeated frame (which we saw), it was obvious.

In another video case, we needed to see why audio and video were not perfectly synchronized; we had a "lip-synch" problem. We built a program that simultaneously made a clicking sound and changed an area of the screen from white to black. When we fed that into the audio-video synchronizer, we could easily see where the audio and video became "un-lip-synched"—the big sound and video changes were obvious in the streams, even after being highly compressed.

In the old days of the Motorola 6800 microprocessor, instruction code DD caused the processor to go into an endless loop, reading from each memory address in order. (Other engineers referred to this as the "Halt and Catch Fire" (HCF) instruction, but we remembered the code by calling it the "Drop Dead" instruction.) Drop Dead mode was wonderful for spotting hardware timing and address logic problems with a scope; all of the address and clock lines were nice, cycling square waves. ▧

When you inject known input patterns, of course, you should be careful that you don't change the bug by setting up new conditions. If the bug is pattern dependent, putting in an artificial pattern may hide the problem. "Make It Fail" before proceeding.

## Start with the Bad

Many systems have several streams that join together, much as tributaries feed into a main river. You could spend a lot of time looking at the wrong tributaries if you started searching at the headwaters. Don't do that. Don't start at the good end and confirm things that are correct; there are too many correct things (or so you hope). Start at the bad end, where the smelly pink goo is, and work your way upstream. Use branch points as test points, and if the problem is still upstream, look up each branch a little way to figure out which one has the problem.

Suppose your furnace doesn't come on. You might guess that you're out of fuel, since that's common, and check that the tank is full. It is. If you decide to verify that you don't have a fuel flow problem—by working your way down, making sure that there's flow through all the feeder pipes, and eventually proving that the spray head has oil squirting out of it—you'll have wasted lots of time (and gotten your hands all oily, too). But you're smart, and you've read this book, so you start at the furnace end, and you quickly confirm that the fuel is fine but the electricity is not. You work your way up to the control box and find several possible tributaries: the main power, the thermostat, and the fire safety override. You could go to the breaker panel to check the main power, but a meter at the control box tells you there's power, so you ignore that tributary. You could go take apart the thermostat, but a meter at the control box tells you it's calling for heat properly, so you ignore that tributary. You could go look at the fire safety breaker, and you do, because a meter at the control box tells you it has tripped. Besides, it's right there over your head, bolted to the hot air duct at the hottest spot, right next to the furnace. So you call the plumber to replace the one-shot fuse and move the sensor to someplace that gets hot only when there's actually a fire.

In the motion estimation story, the badness was the less-than-beautiful output video. The immediate branch above the output was motion estimation versus picture coding. We chose motion estimation, and we were right; the system wasn't finding all the motion. If we had seen lots of colored indicators in all directions of motion, we would have looked at the picture coding branch instead of working our way up the motion estimation branch. In any case, we didn't start at the top and verify the picture coding; that would have involved verifying the frequency domain transform, the run-length coding, the variable-length coding, the quantization, and a dozen other complicated-sounding areas of the software that feed into the picture-coding branch. In fact, they really *are* complicated, so they would have been hard to verify. Furthermore, they were working okay, so all that complicated verification effort would have been wasted.

## Fix the Bugs You Know About

Sometimes, as hard as it might be to believe, there's more than one bug in a system, as in our hotel reservation example. This makes it harder to isolate each bug using "Divide and Conquer." So when you do figure out one of several simultaneous problems, fix it right away, before you look for the others. I've often heard someone say, "Well, that's broken, but it couldn't *possibly* affect the problem we're trying to find." Guess what—it can, and it often does. If you fix something that you know is wrong, you get a clean look at the other issues. Our hotel technician was able to see the direction of the bad wiring on the really slow terminal only after he fixed the high resistances in both directions in the breakout box.

Sometimes, fixing one problem *does* fix the other problem; the two really are the same bug.

Furthermore, if the fix for any problem has *any* effect on *any-*

*thing* else, you'll want to implement it before you continue your testing. If the effect of the fix is to break something else, you'll figure it out sooner and have more time to deal with the new problem.

## Fix the Noise First

A corollary to the previous rule is that certain kinds of bugs are *likely* to cause other bugs, so you should look for and fix them first. In hardware, noisy signals cause all kinds of hard-to-find, intermittent problems. Glitches and ringing on clocks, noise on analog signals, jittery timing, and bad voltage levels need to be taken care of before you look at other problems; the other problems are often very unpredictable and go away when you fix the noise. In software, bad multithread synchronization, accidentally reentrant routines, and uninitialized variables inject that extra shot of randomness that can make your job hell.

But don't get carried away. If you only suspect that noise is the issue, or if the timing is close, weigh the difficulty of fixing the problem against the likelihood that it really is affecting something. When our junior engineers made a new board to fix timing, they only suspected that the timing was a problem, and the fix was very difficult. It merely delayed the real investigation. It's also easy to become a perfectionist and start "fixing" every instance of bad design practice you find, in the interest of general quality. You can eliminate the GOTOs in your predecessor's code simply because you consider them nasty, but if they aren't actually causing problems, you're usually better off leaving them alone.

## Remember

### Divide and Conquer

It's hard for a bug to keep hiding when its hiding place keeps getting cut in half.

- **Narrow the search with successive approximation.** Guess a number from 1 to 100, in seven guesses.

- **Get the range.** If the number is 135 and you think the range is 1 to 100, you'll have to widen the range.

- **Determine which side of the bug you are on.** If there's goo, the pipe is upstream. If there's no goo, the pipe is downstream.

- **Use easy-to-spot test patterns.** Start with clean, clear water so the goo is obvious when it enters the stream.

- **Start with the bad.** There are too many good parts to verify. Start where it's broken and work your way back up to the cause.

- **Fix the bugs you know about.** Bugs defend and hide one another. Take 'em out as soon as you find 'em.

- **Fix the noise first.** Watch for stuff that you *know* will make the rest of the system go crazy. But don't get carried away on marginal problems or aesthetic changes.

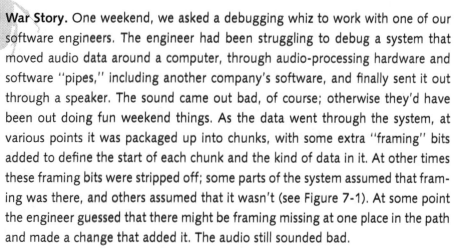

chapter

# 7

# Change One Thing at a Time

"They say that genius is an infinite capacity for taking pains. It's a very bad definition, but it does apply to detective work."

—SHERLOCK HOLMES, *A STUDY IN SCARLET*

**War Story.** One weekend, we asked a debugging whiz to work with one of our software engineers. The engineer had been struggling to debug a system that moved audio data around a computer, through audio-processing hardware and software "pipes," including another company's software, and finally sent it out through a speaker. The sound came out bad, of course; otherwise they'd have been out doing fun weekend things. As the data went through the system, at various points it was packaged up into chunks, with some extra "framing" bits added to define the start of each chunk and the kind of data in it. At other times these framing bits were stripped off; some parts of the system assumed that framing was there, and others assumed that it wasn't (see Figure 7-1). At some point the engineer guessed that there might be framing missing at one place in the path and made a change that added it. The audio still sounded bad.

The whiz came in to help and immediately insisted that they put known data through the pipes and watch for the failure, using instrumentation. It took a while to come up with the right test patterns and to look in the right places, but they

Figure 7-1. An Audio Distortion Generator.

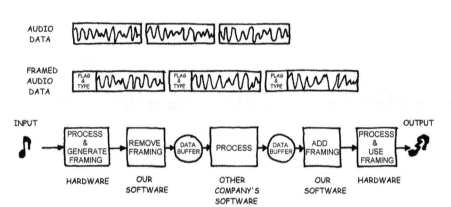

finally saw the data getting clobbered and traced the cause to a buffer pointer error. They fixed the bug, saw that the test pattern went through the trouble spot okay, and with quiet confidence tried it out on real audio data. It *still* sounded bad.

They sat, confused, and began to relook at the data stream. Maybe they had done the fix wrong? Maybe the fix wasn't really in? They spent an hour reconfirming that the fix they had done really did fix a problem. They returned to the code to reconfirm that they were running the fix, and at that point the engineer slapped his forehead. "I changed a handler to add framing. It didn't fix anything, but I never changed it back!" It turned out that the downstream processors thought this extra framing was more audio data, and just played it. It sounded bad. The engineer removed the previous "fix," and the system worked perfectly. The whiz quoted the "Change One Thing at a Time" rule and passed the story along for inclusion in this book. ▧

Our software engineer made a change to try to fix the problem, but when it didn't fix the problem, he assumed that it had no effect. This was a really bad assumption—it did have an effect; it clobbered the audio. It's just that audio clobbered twice doesn't sound much worse than audio clobbered once. When the original clobber was finally removed, his clobber was still there, and audio clobbered once sounds bad, too. When his change didn't fix the problem, he should have backed it out immediately.

Suppose you try to take your wife's car to work one day, but it doesn't start. You notice that it's in Park, and you guess that maybe it has to be in Neutral to start, so you shift to Neutral and try again. It still doesn't start. You sheepishly ask your wife what's up with the car, and she tells you the key is finicky and you have to turn it really far. You twist it hard, almost enough to break it off, and the car *still* doesn't start. It would have started if you had shifted back to Park before trying that manly key twist technique.

## Use a Rifle, Not a Shotgun

Change one thing at a time. You've heard of the shotgun approach? Forget it. Get yourself a good rifle. You'll be a lot better at fixing bugs. I've known technicians trying to fix a bad board who just started swapping components; they might change three or four things and discover, hey, it works now. That's kind of cool, except that they have absolutely no idea which part was the bad one. Worse, all that hacking can break other things that were fine to begin with.

Besides, if you *really saw* exactly what was failing, you'd need to fix only that one thing. In other words, if you think you need a shotgun to hit the target, the problem is that you can't see the target clearly. What you really need is better light and new glasses.

Social scientists and medical researchers often use siblings, and sometimes twins, to isolate the factors they're studying. They might look at identical twins who have been separated, since these twins are genetically identical and any differences come from environmental factors. Similarly, they might look at adopted children, using the family environment as a constant and assuming that any differences come from genetics. When your dentist is trying to find that cold-sensitive tooth, he aims a rifle-like stream of cold air at one tooth at a time; he doesn't fill your mouth with ice chips. And in the days of series-wired Christmas tree bulbs, where the whole string went out if one bulb died, you changed one bulb at a time until the string lit up again—if you changed them all, you'd have an expensive handful of used bulbs with one unidentified bad one in it.

This is just scientific method; in order to see the effect of one variable, the scientist tries to control all of the other variables that might affect the outcome. In the popular grade school plant growth experiment, you use identical soil, an identical watering schedule, and identical seeds, but you vary the amount of light that the plants get. Thus, any variation in plant size is due to sunlight time. If you give them all the same amount of sun, but you vary the amount of water, any variation is due to the amount of water. If small plant size is the bug you want to fix, and you change the pot color and the watering schedule and the sunlight exposure, you won't figure out that pot color has nothing to do with your problem.

If you're working on a mortgage calculation program that seems to be messing up on occasional loans, pin down the loan amount and the term, and vary the interest rate to see that the program does the right thing. If that works, pin down the term and interest rate, and vary the loan amount. If that works, vary just the term. You'll either find the problem in your calculation or discover something really surprising like a math error in your Pentium processor. ("But *that* can't happen!") This kind of surprise happens with the more complex bugs; that's what makes them complex. Isolating and controlling variables is kind of like putting known data into the system: It helps you see the surprises.

**War Story.** I was writing software for a third-party device to capture video from a laptop's VGA output so it could be transmitted and displayed on another computer. Since laptop VGA signals have varied resolution and timing, and have no clock signal to tell you what's going on, you have to sample the video picture coming at you and, by looking at where the edges of the video (surrounded by black) show up, figure out how many pixels the image is, how fast the clock is, and where exactly the edge of each pixel is compared to the capture board's clock.

This was difficult, since each measurement involved setting up a timing guess, measuring the results against it, and then using those results to recalculate the timing for guessing the next parameter. When I first ran the system, it failed miserably, of course. (We always give it a shot, though, don't we?) The interaction between each measurement and the timing for the next measurement made it difficult to analyze the results, but the problem seemed to be determining where the pixel edges were with respect to my clock.

I ran my procedure again, but with all measurements bypassed and set to default values, except for the pixel sample point delay (phase) parameter. This I manually moved through each of eight positions (see Figure 7-2). When the sample point crossed from one input pixel to the next, the system would be sampling the video one clock earlier. I expected the output video to jump one pixel to the left; instead, it jumped right at one phase, then jumped back to the left again at

### Figure 7-2. Finding the Pixel's Edge.

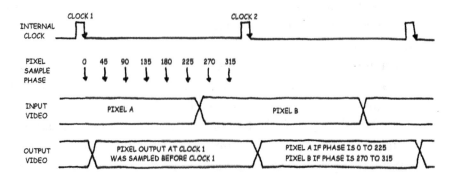

a later phase. This made no sense, but since there were no other variables changing, I knew it was really happening.

   I presented the data to the third-party vendor; the vendor looked into the
problem and discovered that the phase parameter I was using had been misdocu-
mented. As I increased the parameter from 0 to 359, instead of the actual sample
phase going from 0 to 359 degrees as documented, it went from 0 to 89 degrees,
then jumped back to $-270$ degrees, and then went forward to $-1$ degree. The
video jumped right when the phase jumped backward, then jumped left when it
later recrossed the pixel boundary on its way to the starting position again. ▪

I would never have believed that the phase parameter was faulty
if I hadn't pinned down everything but the phase, and then varied it
through known values. Since the phase was the only thing that was
changing, it *had* to be the cause of the jump.

## Grab the Brass Bar with Both Hands

In many cases, you'll want to change different parts of the system to
see if they affect the problem. This usually should be a warning that
you're guessing rather than using your instrumentation well enough
to see what's going on. You're changing conditions instead of looking
for the failure as it occurs naturally. This can hide the first problem
and cause more. It's exactly what our software engineer did wrong
with the audio framing.

   On nuclear-powered subs, there's a brass bar in front of the control panel for the power plant. When status alarms begin to go off,
the engineers are trained to grab the brass bar with both hands and
hold on until they've looked at all the dials and indicators, and understand exactly what's going on in the system. What this does is
help them overcome the temptation to start "fixing" things, throw-

ing switches and opening valves. These quick fixes confuse the automatic recovery systems, bury the original fault beneath an onslaught
of new conditions, and may cause a real, major disaster. It's more
effective to remember to do something ("Grab the bar!") than to
remember *not* to do something ("Don't touch that dial!"). So, grab
the bar!

**War Story.** At a Christmas party at our fraternity house one year, a brother (ap-
propriately nicknamed "The Bungler") set up his stereo system in the living room
to provide festive holiday music. He ran the wire to the right speaker along the
wall, and when he got to the fireplace (which no one ever used, even though it
had logs freshly arranged and ready for a fire), he ran the wires behind the logs.
Sure enough, at some point in the evening, someone lit the fire, and soon thereafter, to the warm glow of a Yule blaze, the right speaker shut off. The insulation
on the wires had melted and shorted out the right channel of the amplifier, blowing the right channel fuse. The brothers didn't think of this, however, and with
dates hanging on their arms and eggnog dancing in their heads, they were not
about to break out meters or look at fuses. They decided to see whether the
problem was the speaker or the amplifier, so they swapped the wires at the amplifier between the right and left speakers. When they turned on the amplifier, of
course, the left channel was shorted out and the left fuse blew. Now neither
speaker worked, and the party was without music. Bah! Humbug! They'd have
been better off if they'd stayed at the eggnog bar (and held on with both
hands). ■

## Change One Test at a Time

Sometimes, changing the test sequence or some operating parameter makes a problem occur more regularly; this helps you see the

failure and may be a great clue to what's going on. But you should still change only one thing at a time so that you can tell exactly which parameter had the effect. And if a change doesn't seem to have an effect, back it out right away!

## Compare with a Good One

Once you have a way to make a system fail or not (even if it's just random), you have a wonderful opportunity to be a differencing engine. (Be a differencing engine! See the world! Or, at least, see the differences!) Using two cases, one that failed and one that didn't, compare scope traces, code traces, debug output, status windows, or whatever else you can instrument. I've found many bugs simply by looking at two debug logs side by side, one of a case where the system worked and one where it didn't, and noting the difference between them. "Wow! Look at that! The videophone call that worked set the phone number field to 1-700-VID-TEST as expected, but the one that failed somehow set it to 1-700-BAD-JEST."

If you've made a whole bunch of code changes between the two tests or set up a different scenario for the two tests, then the tests will be hard to compare; you'll constantly have to account for differences that aren't due to the bug. You want to narrow down the differences between those two traces to *only the bug*. Get all that other stuff out of there. Try to get both logs from the same machine on consecutive tries—don't use different machines, different software, different parameters, different user input, different days, or different environments. Don't even wear a different shirt; it just might hide the bug. (Don't laugh; there's a war story in the next chapter in which the pattern of my shirt was a key factor.)

That's not to say you shouldn't instrument things that aren't related to the bug. You don't really know what's related to the bug yet, so you want all the instrumentation you can get. And if it's not re-lated to the bug, it'll come out the same on both logs. Yes, you'll have to paw through a whole bunch of irrelevant data, but the same irrelevant data will be in both logs, and you can skim right over it. In Chapter 4, "Make It Fail," I talked about seeing the failure in the difference between captured logs of a good video call and a bad one; we didn't know what we were looking for, so we had to filter through a lot of similar stuff to see the surprise command in the bad call.

Okay, this isn't as easy as it sounds. I've often been asked to explain how I do it—look at a couple of logs and spot what the prob-lem is. I've been asked to teach a course for entry-level testers on how to do it. I've been asked to write a software filter that will read a log automatically and find the bad stuff. But finding the bad stuff isn't something you can teach a beginner or write a program to do. What you're looking for is never the same as last time. And it takes a fair amount of knowledge and intelligence to sift through the irrele-vant differences, differences that were caused by timing or other fac-tors. This knowledge is beyond what a beginner has, and this intelligence is beyond what software can do. (A.I. waved good-bye, remember?) The most that software can do is help you to format and filter logs so that when you apply your superior human brain (you *do* have a superior one, don't you?) to analyzing the logs, the differ-ences (and possibly the cause of the differences) will jump right out at that brain.

When you look at a long, complex log, you'll be tempted to look at suspect areas only, and that's fine if you find something right away. But if you don't, be prepared to look at the whole log—you don't know where the difference will show up.

And I have to warn you: This is probably the most mind-numb-ingly boring task you will ever have to do. Grab a strong cup of coffee, prop your eyelids open with toothpicks, and slog your way through it. (On second thought, forget the toothpicks. You could put an eye out with those things!)

## What Did You Change Since the
## Last Time It Worked?

**War Story.** In my college years I worked in a furniture shop, and one day a co-worker said, "Hey, you're from MIT. You probably know all about stereos; maybe you can fix my problem." Well, I didn't really know all about stereos, but I used them, and I thought I might be able to help. She told me she had just taken her turntable in for repair and now it sounded terrible. (For you youngsters, a turntable is a record player. It plays those big black vinyl discs that come in cardboard sleeves and actually have music on both sides.) She noted that the repair shop had replaced the cartridge (which generates the electrical signal from the needle that rides on the record). We went over to her place to check it out; she played a record, and it indeed sounded terrible. In fact, it reminded me of the time I plugged a portable tape deck into an amplifier and turned the tape deck volume up too loud for the amplifier input to handle—it sounded very harsh and distorted. "Input volume too loud" was the first thing that came to my mind.

I knew (because she told me) that a change had been made since the last time it sounded good: The cartridge had been replaced. I also knew from setting up stereos that there were two kinds of cartridges, magnetic and ceramic, and that they usually had two different types of inputs on the back of the amplifier (see Figure 7-3). This was because one of them was *louder* than the other. The problem seemed pretty clear to me: She had switched from a low-volume cartridge to a high-volume one, but she plugged it into the same place she had plugged it into before, and now it was overdriving the input.

I didn't know which kind of cartridge was which, but I figured that switching the cable would do the job. I looked around the back of the stereo and found, to

Figure 7-3. How We Played Music in the Old Days.

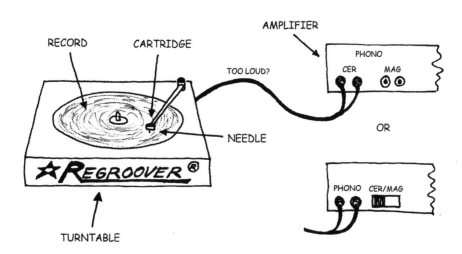

my delight, that it was even easier than that: There was a switch. I flipped it, and immediately the music sounded great. In fact, since she had just gotten a brand new needle and cartridge, it sounded better than it had ever sounded before. Total analysis time: about thirty seconds. Total resulting apparent godlike technical prowess: huge. (Total resulting amorous liaisons: zero. Oh, well, godlike technical prowess just wasn't hot in those pre-dot.com days.) ▨

Sometimes the difference between a working system and a broken one is that a design change was made. When this happens, a good system starts failing. It's very helpful to figure out which version first caused the system to fail, even if this involves going back and testing successively older versions until the failure goes away. Once it does, go forward to the next version and verify that the failure occurs again. Once you've taken that step, you've at least narrowed down the problem to something that changed between those two versions. Of course, you have a complete source design tracking system, so you can very quickly look at all the differences between any two versions. (You do, don't you? If you don't, get one. Now. See the next rule, "Keep an Audit Trail," for more on this.) Assuming that the change was not a complete overhaul of the system, this gives you a very sharp focus on the problem.

Usually, the new design is faulty; that's why we test new designs before shipping them. Sometimes the new design of one section is incompatible with another, perfectly good section. That was the case with the stereo system in the story—the new cartridge was fine, but the amplifier needed to be changed to accommodate it.

Some cases are tricky, though. Sometimes the problem has existed for a long time, but it doesn't show up until something else changes, like the timing or the database size. You may think you've broken it with version 5.0, but in fact what you've done is expose it; it's been broken since version 3.1. Often a new piece of code or a new hardware revision sets up new conditions that make an old, used-to-be-reliable subsystem fail. The subsystem had a hole in it, but you never wandered to where you could fall through it before. You may be tempted to go after the "bug" that leads you to that hole, and this can sometimes be the right short-term fix, but what you really want to do is plug the hole.

**War Story.** After living in an old house for several years, we found water dripping from the first-floor ceiling around the stairs during a late winter rainstorm. I worked my way up trying to find the source of the water, and found myself in the crawl space around the attic, where water was dripping in through the ice-dammed roof. It was running in along one of the rafters, then hitting a credit-card-sized tab of metal that had been driven into the rafter. This deflected the water downward, so that it dripped onto the floor and down through the house. Nearby was an old plastic tub, like you'd put into a sink and soak dishes in. When we moved in, the tub had been directly under the tab, but I had been crawling around in the space over the summer doing wiring and had kicked it out of position, unaware of its purpose.

I had introduced a ''bug'' while working on the wiring: I moved the tub out of position. Of course, I used the obvious short-term fix for the ''bug''—I moved the tub back under the leak. But that was only temporary. The next summer we fixed the real bug that the tub repositioning had only exposed: We had the roof reshingled. ▓

# Remember

## Change One Thing at a Time

You need some predictability in your life. Remove the changes that didn't do what you expected. They probably did something you didn't expect.

- **Isolate the key factor.** Don't change the watering schedule if you're looking for the effect of the sunlight.

- **Grab the brass bar with both hands.** If you try to fix the nuke without knowing what's wrong first, you may have an underwater Chernobyl on your hands.

- **Change one test at a time.** I knew my VGA capture phase was broken because nothing else was changing.

- **Compare it with a good one.** If the bad ones all have something that the good ones don't, you're onto the problem.

- **Determine what you changed since the last time it worked.** My friend had changed the cartridge on the turntable, so that was a good place to start.

chapter

# 8

# Keep an Audit Trail

"There is no branch of detective science which is so important and so much neglected as the art of tracing footsteps."

—SHERLOCK HOLMES, *A STUDY IN SCARLET*

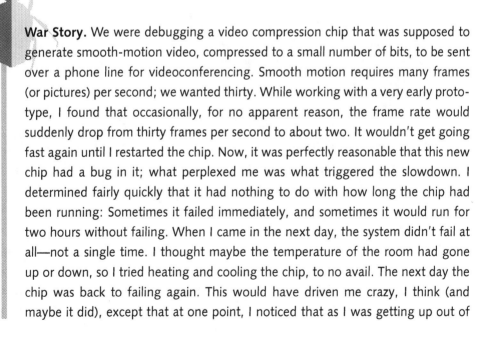

**War Story.** We were debugging a video compression chip that was supposed to generate smooth-motion video, compressed to a small number of bits, to be sent over a phone line for videoconferencing. Smooth motion requires many frames (or pictures) per second; we wanted thirty. While working with a very early prototype, I found that occasionally, for no apparent reason, the frame rate would suddenly drop from thirty frames per second to about two. It wouldn't get going fast again until I restarted the chip. Now, it was perfectly reasonable that this new chip had a bug in it; what perplexed me was what triggered the slowdown. I determined fairly quickly that it had nothing to do with how long the chip had been running: Sometimes it failed immediately, and sometimes it would run for two hours without failing. When I came in the next day, the system didn't fail at all—not a single time. I thought maybe the temperature of the room had gone up or down, so I tried heating and cooling the chip, to no avail. The next day the chip was back to failing again. This would have driven me crazy, I think (and maybe it did), except that at one point, I noticed that as I was getting up out of my chair, it suddenly failed. I sat down, restarted the processor, watched it run fast, then got up out of my chair; it failed again. Maybe it was lonely and didn't want me to leave?

I realized that getting up out of the chair added more of my shirt to the camera's field of view. Now, I'm from New Hampshire, and I was wearing (as I often do) a plaid flannel shirt. The previous day, I had worn a plain blue shirt. The day before that, I had worn another plaid flannel shirt. A few more experiments showed me that, sure enough, when the video compressor tried to handle an extremely difficult-to-compress pattern (the moving plaid shirt), it pretty much threw up its hands and quit trying (see Figure 8-1).

**Figure 8-1. Video Compression Versus New Hampshire Flannel.**

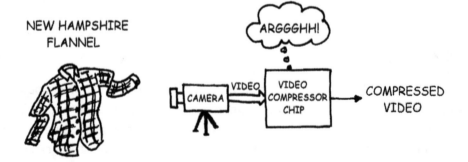

My colleagues and the vendor of the compressor chip found it hard to believe that a shirt could do that, but it was very easy to prove. (In fact, I often used those plaid shirts to demonstrate that clothing can push video compression engines to the limit—another useful marketing tool developed while debugging.)

I confess that I didn't write down what shirt I was wearing each day, so I didn't keep a written audit trail during the testing. I didn't write down the fact that my standing up was what caused the processor to fail. I just remembered both of these things; they were pretty easy to remember. But when I sent the report to the chip vendor, I did write down that the plaid shirt mattered, that standing up in front of the camera in the plaid shirt made the chip fail, and that the chip had to be restarted if it was to recover. I even sent a photocopy of the shirt pattern so the vendor could re-create the problem. (The vendor actually asked for the shirt off my back, but I wouldn't give it up.) Imagine how much more useful that was than if I had written, "Chip occasionally slows down and needs restarting to speed back up again," or even, "Chip fails occasionally." (I've actually received bug reports that essentially just say, "It's broken.") ■

The point of this story is that sometimes it's the most insignificant-seeming thing that's actually the key to making a bug happen. What seems insignificant to the person doing the testing (the plaid shirt) may be important to the person trying to fix the problem. And what seems obvious to the tester (the chip had to be restarted) may be completely missed by the fixer. So you have to take note of everything—on the off chance that it might be important and nonobvious.

## Write Down What You Did, in What Order, and What Happened

Keep an audit trail. As you investigate a problem, write down what you did, what order you did it in, and what happened as a result. Do this every time. It's just like instrumenting the software or the hardware—you're instrumenting the test sequence. You have to be able to see what each step was, and what the result was, to determine which step to focus on during debugging.

**War Story.** A customer kept calling customer support reporting that a floppy disk would work just once, then fail after that. Customer support kept mailing out new copies, but each of them worked once, then failed. Finally, the support people got a live audit trail by having the customer call and give a play-by-play of the process. The floppy worked the first time, as expected, and then the customer put it away—by sticking it to the filing cabinet *with a magnet*. ■

When you have a food allergy, allergists will try to determine what food causes it by asking you to associate what you ate with the reaction. If the connection is subtle and they need more detail, they may have you keep a diary of everything you eat and every reaction you have. This is an audit trail, plain and simple. It gives them a way to find the correlation between eating strawberries and breaking out in hives. (The fix is obvious: Don't eat strawberries.)

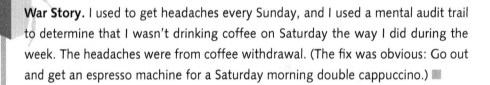

**War Story.** I used to get headaches every Sunday, and I used a mental audit trail to determine that I wasn't drinking coffee on Saturday the way I did during the week. The headaches were from coffee withdrawal. (The fix was obvious: Go out and get an espresso machine for a Saturday morning double cappuccino.) ■

When you go for psychoanalysis, the doctor tries to extract an audit trail of your life (what happened and how you felt/feel about it) to figure out why you're so messed up. Imagine how many session fees you could save if you could just hand the shrink your detailed biography! (I know, I know, it doesn't really work like that. The fact is, debugging a neurotic person is nearly impossible because the instrumentation is faulty—it forgets, suppresses, and lies—and you can't just go in and fix the problem—you have to talk it into fixing itself.)

## The Devil Is in the Details

Unfortunately, while the value of an audit trail is often accepted, the level of detail required is not, so a lot of important information gets left out. What kind of system was running? What was the sequence of events leading up to the failure? And sometimes even, what *was* the actual failure? (Duh!) Sometimes the report just says, "It's broken." It doesn't say that the graphics were completely garbled or that all the red areas came up green or that the third number was wrong. It just says it failed.

Wait. It gets worse. In order to get details, we insist that the person reporting the bug capture debug logs of the failure. So now we get a bug report and three logs. Do they say which one is the failure? No. Do they tell us what the symptoms were? No. "It's all in the log." Well, the instrumentation is in the log, but what the tester saw and didn't like is not.

Imagine keeping your food allergy diary, but writing down only what you ate and not that you broke out in hives. The allergist would be helpless. The key is to annotate any debug traces or logs that you have with any conditions and symptoms that aren't actually in the log. If you can correlate symptoms to time stamps, that's even better; see the next section, "Correlate."

Be specific and consistent in describing things. In video communications, we often have system A and system B and sometimes even system C, all trying to talk to each other. We'll get a bug report that says, "No remote video." Is the remote side system A or system B? And is it the video displayed *on* the remote side or the video being sent *from* the remote side that didn't happen? You can't even begin to figure out the problem until you have the basic symptoms straight.

Another detail to note is not just what happened, but how much. For example, in videoconferencing, where the interaction between various vendors' equipment can cause minor noises during connection and disconnection, it's important to note how long a sound lasts and how annoying it is. A "half-second burst of barely audible hum" might be safely ignored, whereas a "six-second, painfully ear-piercing shriek" probably needs looking into.

If you took basic high school chemistry, you may remember the classic "describe a candle" lab. You had to write down fifty unique things about a candle. After you struggled with the list for a while, they gave you some hints—the main one was, "Give the reader enough information to accurately understand the experience." Details! It's not enough to say that the candle gives off heat and light when you ignite the wick—how much heat and light? Should a person who re-creates your experiment hide in a bunker when he detonates the candle? "It's hot enough that you can hold your hand flat, six inches above the flame, for only two seconds before you have to pull your hand away." Ah; no bunker required.

**War Story.** An acquaintance of mine was working on a hardware project. He happened to touch the case of the power supply and felt a faint electrical buzz (in other words, a mild shock). Along with catching fire, electrocuting people is one of those bad things for a hardware product to do, so he looked into it. He wasn't sure if what he was feeling was really a shock or just the normal audible hum, so he convinced an associate to touch the power supply. Nothing. My friend tried again, and again he felt the shock. He convinced a few others to try it, and none of them felt the electricity. He still did. They were standing around with their hands on their hips, ready to take him to the loony bin, when they noticed he wasn't wearing shoes. They all were, and their shoes insulated them from the ground well enough to avoid the shock. And while he may rightfully be accused of being insane for working in a hardware lab with bare feet, he wasn't hallucinating about the bug. ■

Like the folks with the car that only liked vanilla and chocolate ice cream, the key was in a detail you would ordinarily never suspect. But you've read this book, so now you suspect and take note of *every-thing.*

## Correlate

Correlating symptoms with other symptoms or debug information is very useful. "It made a really loud noise just after I connected" is better than "It made a really loud noise." But, "It made a really loud noise for four seconds starting at 14:05:23" is the best. With that information, when I look at a debug log and see a pair of audio control commands at 14:05:23 and 14:05:27, I have a pretty good idea that those commands have something to do with the problem.

Back to your food allergy diary again: Imagine writing down what and when you ate on one sheet, and that you got hives on another. But you don't write down *when* you got hives. Again, your allergist is helpless.

In systems where multiple devices communicate, keep traces of both systems, with time stamps that are well synchronized. This is really useful information. It's possible to look at two logs from two different machines that were trying to talk to each other and men-tally subtract a minute and twenty-three seconds from one of them because its clock was that far ahead of the other one, but it's difficult and annoying. So take a moment to set them all to the same time.

One last trip to the allergy analogy: Imagine keeping your eating diary on London time and your symptom diary on San Francisco time. Your allergist won't be helpless but may become as irritated as you are.

Many bugs have been found by correlating symptoms with human timetables:

**War Story.** A problem with garbage characters proved to be correlated with the times that Fred was on duty. It turns out that Fred had a big gut, which would press on the keyboard when he reached up for the coffeepot.

In another story, a crash was correlated with the times that George was on duty. The cause of the crash was a text buffer overrun. George had figured out a way to type twice as much detail into the comment field: He would type a line's worth into the teletype keyboard, but before he got to the end, he would grab the print head and push it back to the left. The program depended on the mechanical auto-carriage-return to limit the input.

The computer center crash I described in Chapter 4, "Make It Fail," was correlated with the vending machine activity during the 3 P.M. coffee break. ▪

## Audit Trails for Design Are Also Good for Testing

In Chapter 7, "Change One Thing at a Time," I mentioned source code control systems. These are databases of program and tool files that allow you to re-create any given version of your software, well after later versions have been created. These systems keep engineers who are working on the same project from clobbering each other's changes as they code in their own. (Unfortunately, they don't keep them from clobbering good, working code.) They also give you an audit trail of your design, so you can tell what changes were made when, and get back to a known state of your product if necessary. This is good for the design process, but even better for the debug process. When a bug shows up in a particular version of a system, you have a record of all the changes that were made since the last time the system worked. If everything else is the same, knowing exactly what code changes broke the product gives you a real head start on fixing them.

Source code control systems are now being called "configuration control systems" because they don't just track your program code;

they also track the tools you use to build the program. Tool control is critical to the accurate re-creation of a version, and you should make sure you have it. As discussed later, unrecognized tool variations can cause some very strange effects.

## The Shortest Pencil Is Longer Than the Longest Memory

Never trust your memory with a detail—write it down. If you trust your memory, a number of things will happen. You'll forget the details that you didn't think were important at the time, and those, of course, will prove to be the critical ones. You'll forget the details that actually weren't important to you, but might be important to someone else working on a different problem later. You won't be able to transmit information to anyone else except verbally, which wastes everybody's time, assuming you're still around to talk about it. And you won't be able to remember *exactly* how things happened and in what order and how events related to one another, all of which is crucial information.

Write it down. It's better to write it electronically so you can make backup copies, attach it to bug reports, distribute it to others easily, and maybe even filter it with automated analysis tools later. Write down what you did and what happened as a result. Save your debug logs and traces, and annotate them with related events and effects that they don't inherently record themselves. Write down your theories and your fixes. Write it all down.

"The horror of that moment," the King went on, "I shall never, *never* forget!" "You will, though," the Queen said, "if you don't make a memorandum of it."

—LEWIS CARROLL,
*THROUGH THE LOOKING GLASS*

# Remember

### Keep an Audit Trail

Better yet, don't remember "Keep an Audit Trail." Write down "Keep an Audit Trail."

- **Write down what you did, in what order, and what happened as a result.** When did you last drink coffee? When did the headache start?

- **Understand that any detail could be the important one.** It had to be a plaid shirt to crash the video chip.

- **Correlate events.** "It made a noise for four seconds starting at 21:04:53" is better than "It made a noise."

- **Understand that audit trails for design are also good for testing.** Software configuration control tools can tell you which revision introduced the bug.

- **Write it down!** No matter how horrible the moment, make a memorandum of it.

chapter

9

# Check the Plug

"There is nothing more deceptive than an obvious fact."

—SHERLOCK HOLMES, *THE BOSCOMBE VALLEY MYSTERY*

**War Story.** In June 1984 my family moved into a ninety-year-old house and quickly became familiar with the hodgepodge of systems that kept it running. Everything was dual, it seemed, starting with the dual electric service for the apartment upstairs (along with wiring quirks that I'll discuss later). There were dual furnaces driving the forced hot water heating system, one wood burning, which the previous owner had used for primary heat, and one oil burning, which he had used for backup and which I decided to use for primary heat. (They say that burning wood heats you three times: when you split it, when you stack it, and when you burn it. The most effort I intended to expend was twisting the thermostat dial.) There were even dual septic systems and dual wells.

The hot water heater was a small heat exchanger that transferred heat from the main hot water heating system to the sink and shower hot water plumbing (see Figure 9-1). That was unfortunate because you had to run the furnace all summer, but that wasn't the problem that bothered me. Cold showers bothered me.

It seemed that any use of water anywhere in the house would drop the hot water pressure, and I'd be scrubbing my goose bumps. I looked into fancy self-

Figure 9-1. A Unique Heat and Hot Water System.

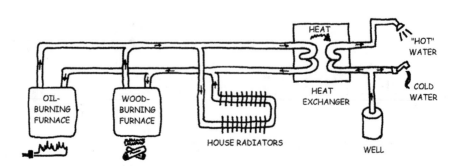

adjusting valves that would keep the temperature stable, but they were too expensive. A friend of mine (a mechanical engineer) suggested that I just needed a pressure-balanced valve—and I discovered that I already had one. I started to think I just wasn't getting enough hot water.

The system was "instantaneous," meaning that it heats the water as you use it, rather than storing it in a tank. You're not supposed to be able to run out. So I guessed that the water wasn't set hot enough—but no, the thermostat on the exchanger was set to 140°, hot enough for the dishwasher. The thermometer on the exchanger showed that the water was indeed 140°, and whenever the water dropped below 140°, the source hot water pump (from the furnace system) would kick in. The problem was that it couldn't keep the temperature up through a hot shower, and it took a long time to recover afterward. I thought maybe this instantaneous water heater idea wasn't so hot, and considered getting a new one.

By now it was late autumn, and in New England that means cold weather. We found that the heating system couldn't warm the house up very quickly in the morning. Granted, forced hot water isn't as responsive as forced hot air, but this was really sluggish. I felt the radiator tubes when the heat was on, and they weren't very hot. So I went downstairs and looked at the thermostat on the oil furnace boiler. It was set to 165°.

A good forced hot water furnace setting is 190°; what I had was a forced *warm* water furnace. I found that the previous owner had set the wood burner to

190° and the oil burner to 165°, undoubtedly so the oil would kick in only if the wood burner stopped heating. That's fine for a backup, but not for a primary. I set it to 190°, and the house was able to warm right up.

Not only that, but the hot water heater started working right, too. Its heat exchanger was now drawing heat from a 190° source, instead of a 165° source. You know, somebody's Nth Law of Thermodynamics says that you can't heat water to 140° in a heat exchanger with a 165° source—at least, not fast enough to run a good, long, hot shower.

My mistake, as I puzzled over the problem, shivering in the shower, was that I assumed there was a good source of heat for the exchanger. In the parlance of the "Divide and Conquer" rule, I limited my range too tightly and missed the real problem. This is more likely to happen with what I call "overhead" or "foundation" factors. Because they're general requirements (electricity, heat, clock), they get overlooked when you debug the details.

Granted, it was a strange circumstance that created the forced warm water system, but there are many strange circumstances out there, and if you ignore the possibility, you're sure to be rudely awakened sometime. Like by a cold shower.

## Question Your Assumptions

Never trust your assumptions, especially when they're at the heart of some unexplainable problem. Ask yourself the age-old stupid question: "Is it plugged in?" This seems like a silly thing, but it happens a lot. You go crazy trying to figure out why your modem software is broken and it turns out you kicked out the phone plug. Remember my friend with the in-sink hot water heater? He assumed that the thing had power from the breaker and spent a futile, painful after-noon under the sink.

More often, it happens at a lower level. You're wondering why some fancy digital chip isn't working correctly and you haven't looked to see whether you've actually got power to it. Does it have a clock? Your graphics hardware doesn't work. Is the right graphics driver installed on the system? Are you running in the right operating system? Is the feature enabled in the registry? Are you even running the code you think you're running? It's classic to say, "Hmm, this new code works just like the old code" and then find out that, in fact, you didn't actually load the new code. You loaded the old code, or you loaded the new code but it's still executing the old code because you didn't reboot your computer or you left an easier-to-find copy of the old code on your system.

When we look at a problem, we often find trouble in a particular place, but the cause of that trouble is somewhere upstream of that place, or in its basic foundation. The conditions for proper operation are not there, and this makes for some very bizarre behavior. At some point when you run into a problem that seems completely other-worldly, stop and check to see that you're actually on the right planet.

In the VGA capture story a few chapters back, I narrowed the problem down to a vendor's function that was not acting as docu-mented. I didn't assume that the function worked in the face of evi-dence to the contrary—I contacted the vendor, and the vendor admitted that the function was broken.

Suppose you turned on the TV and the picture was snowy. You wouldn't dive right in and try to fix your TV; you'd first question whether you were actually receiving a good picture. Is your VCR se-lected and driving channel 3, and you're tuned to channel 7? Or is your antenna aimed at East Snowshoe, Vermont, which has only one UHF station? Is your cable company down again? Maybe you're just watching a mid-December Cheese Bay Packers game. But you can bet it's not the TV, and that's fortunate, because the TV has no user-serviceable parts inside and you didn't go for the three-year deluxe maintenance contract that the kid at Best Buy tried to sell you.

Your soufflé didn't rise. Is the oven on?

Your car won't start. Before you take apart the carburetor, are you out of gas?

## Don't Start at Square Three

Speaking of starting your car, another aspect to consider is whether the start-up conditions are correct. You may have the power plugged in, but did you hit the start button? Has the graphics driver been initialized? Has the chip been reset? Have the registers been programmed correctly? Did you push the primer button on your weed whacker three times? Did you set the choke? *Did you set the on/off switch to on?* (I usually notice this one after six or seven fruitless pulls.)

If you depend on memory being initialized before your program runs, but you don't do it explicitly, it's even worse—*sometimes* start-up conditions *will* be correct. But not when you demo the program to the investors.

## Test the Tool

**War Story.** Early in the days of a multimedia video project, we had a highly paid consultant benchmark a blazing fast (at the time) 33-MHz 486 processor reading and writing video files. We needed a certain speed, and we wanted to see if we could maintain it. The consultant's test programs weren't as quick as we'd hoped, and, curiously, his read program was slower than his write program; this was contrary to our experience and expectation. He worked on the problem for a few weeks, optimizing every single part of the code loop as best he could. Finally, admitting that he didn't really understand why the reads were slower, he turned the results over to us.

We looked at his code and found that he was not explicitly setting the file data type to binary (1s and 0s), but instead was leaving it unspecified. In our software development environment, this meant that the data type was automatically assumed to be text input (letters and numbers). This made the system search the file (while it did the read transfer) for line feeds and carriage returns, in order to substitute new-line characters—the kind of thing that would slow down a read process. We changed the function to explicitly transfer binary, and the read function sped up considerably, to what we expected. When we questioned the consultant about it, he said he assumed that the development system defaulted to binary if the file type was unspecified. But he hadn't checked, and he assumed wrong. ▨

Our consultant, faced with inexplicable behavior, spent weeks and a lot of our money trying to find the bug in code that was perfectly fine. But because he never questioned whether his compiler did what he thought it did, he never figured it out. And he never worked for us again.

Your bad assumptions may not be about the product you're building, but rather about the tools you're using to build it, as in the consultant story. Default settings are a common problem. Building for the wrong environment is another—if you use a Macintosh compiler, you obviously can't run the program on an Intel PC, but what about your libraries and other common code resources? Make sure you have the right ones, and the latest ones. The bugs that arise from mismatched development tools can be truly weird.

It may not be just your assumptions about the tools that are bad—the tools may have bugs, too. (Actually, even this is just your bad assumption that the tool is bug-free. It was built by engineers; why would it be any more trustworthy than what you're building?)

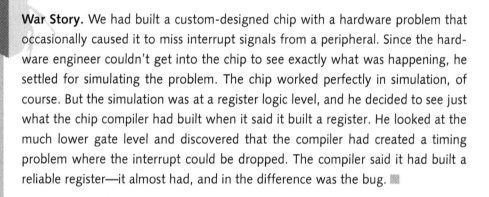

**War Story.** We had built a custom-designed chip with a hardware problem that occasionally caused it to miss interrupt signals from a peripheral. Since the hardware engineer couldn't get into the chip to see exactly what was happening, he settled for simulating the problem. The chip worked perfectly in simulation, of course. But the simulation was at a register logic level, and he decided to see just what the chip compiler had built when it said it built a register. He looked at the much lower gate level and discovered that the compiler had created a timing problem where the interrupt could be dropped. The compiler said it had built a reliable register—it almost had, and in the difference was the bug. ▤

You might also make bad assumptions about debugging tools. When you use a continuity checker with a dead battery to test some connection, it's not going to beep when you test a perfectly good connection, and you'll be fooled into thinking the connection is bad. So the first thing you do is touch the two probes together to make sure it beeps when no test connection is involved at all. You test the test tool. Before you measure signals with an oscilloscope, touch your scope probe with a finger to make sure it's active, and touch it to 5 volts to make sure your vertical scale is right. When you add print statements to a piece of software that prints only if a certain event occurs, you'll never see the event if the print statements don't work. So print a message in any case, and just make it say whether the event occurred or not. If you take your child's temperature and it reads 75°, take another measurement, preferably with a different thermometer. (If the 75° reading persists, let the poor kid out of the freezer.)

**War Story.** After a few months of hot showers in the aforementioned ninety-year-old house, all of a sudden the furnace quit. Since we were now heating with oil, not wood, I realized that our oil delivery schedule was probably too sparse and immediately checked the oil tank gauge. It read one-quarter full. So I called the furnace guy, and he came over that evening to see what he could do. He immediately went to check the oil level, too. Even as I told him that I'd already checked it, he banged the gauge with his flashlight, and it snapped down to zero. He delivered more fuel and pegged me a foolish city slicker. ▪

"Convictions are more dangerous enemies of truth than lies."

—FRIEDRICH NIETZSCHE

# Remember

### Check the Plug

Obvious assumptions are often wrong. And to rub it in, assumption bugs are usually the easiest to fix.

- ▪ **Question your assumptions.** Are you running the right code? Are you out of gas? Is it plugged in?

- ▪ **Start at the beginning.** Did you initialize memory properly? Did you squeeze the primer bulb? Did you turn it on?

- ▪ **Test the tool.** Are you running the right compiler? Is the fuel gauge stuck? Does the meter have a dead battery?

# 10

# Get a Fresh View

"Nothing clears up a case so much as stating it to another person."

—SHERLOCK HOLMES, *SILVER BLAZE*

**War Story.** I had some car trouble—it was so weird that I don't even remember the exact details, but it was something like, whenever I put the car into reverse, the fuse for the brake lights would blow out. I'd gone through several fuses before I figured that much out, and on a whim I mentioned it to an associate of mine who was pretty familiar with car repair. Without hesitating, he said, "The dome light is pinching a wire against the frame of the car. If you open up the dome light, clear it and wrap some electrical tape around it, you'll be fine." I laughed; how could the dome light have anything to do with the brakes? He said it happens all the time (see Figure 10-1).

### Figure 10-1. The Holistic Approach to Car Repair.

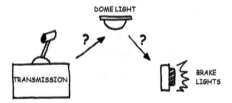

I decided that it was easy enough to humor him, so I went out to my car and unscrewed the dome light cover. Sure enough, there under the dome light bracket was a wire pinched against, and shorted to, the frame. I freed it, wrapped it with black electrical tape, put my car into reverse, and watched my brake lights not burn out. ▦

I could have used all the other rules to figure this one out: I could have read up on the electrical system of the car and probed around the wiring harnesses with a meter. That would have taken time, whereas my associate had experience and knew the answer already. All I had to do was ask for help. It took only a few minutes, and since I was at work, I could even easily "procure" some electrical tape.

## Ask for Help

There are at least three reasons to ask for help, not counting the desire to dump the whole problem into someone else's lap: a fresh view, expertise, and experience. And people are usually willing to help because it gives them a chance to demonstrate how clever they are.

### A Breath of Fresh Insight

It's hard to see the big picture from the bottom of a rut. We're all human. We all have our biases about everything, including where a bug is hiding. Those biases can keep us from seeing what's really going on. Someone who comes at the problem from an unbiased (actually, differently biased) viewpoint can give us great insights and trigger new approaches. If nothing else, that person can at least tell you it looks like you've got a nasty problem there and offer you a shoulder to cry on.

In fact, sometimes *explaining* the problem to someone else gives *you* a fresh view, and you solve the problem yourself. Just organizing the facts forces you out of the rut you were in. I've even heard of a company that has a room with a mannequin in it—you go explain your problems to the mannequin first. I imagine the mannequin is quite useful and contributes to the quick solution of a number of problems. (It's probably more interactive than some people you work with. I bet it's also a very forgiving listener, and none of your regrettable misconceptions will show up in next year's salary review.)

## Ask an Expert

There are occasions where a part of the system is a mystery to us; rather than go to school for a year to learn about it, we can ask an expert and learn what we need to know quickly. But be sure that your expert really is an expert on the subject—if he gives you vague, buzzword-laden theories, he's a technical charlatan and won't be helpful. If he tells you it'll take thirty hours to research and prepare a report, he's a consultant and may be helpful, but at a price.

In any case, experts "Understand the System" better than we do, so they know the road map and can give us great search hints. And when we've found the bug, they can help us design a proper fix that won't mess up the rest of the system.

## The Voice of Experience

You may not have a whole lot of experience, but there may be people around you who have seen this situation before and, given a quick description of what's going on, can tell you exactly what's wrong, like the dome light short in the story. Like experts, people with experi-

ence in a specific area can be hard to find, and thus expensive. It
may be worth the money:

**War Story.** There's an old story about a gentleman who maintained the equipment in a large factory for many years, until he retired. The factory ran fine without him for some time, until one day a machine stopped and would not run again,
despite all the efforts of the new maintenance personnel. They called the retiree,
described the problem, and asked for his help. He said he thought he could fix it,
but it would cost them $10,000. They were desperate, so they agreed.

He came to the factory with his toolbox and went to the machine. He opened
the box, took out a hammer, and whacked the side of the machine once. It started
running. He put the hammer away, closed up the box, and asked for his $10,000.
The factory owners were furious. "$10,000 for one whack with a hammer?"
"No," the retiree corrected them, "$10 for the whack with the hammer. $9,990
for knowing where to whack." ∎

As noted in the introduction, there are troubleshooting guides
available that collect the experience of many troubleshooters for a
particular system. If such a guide is available for the system you're
working on, and it's a "something broke" problem rather than a
"bad design" problem, go for it—you just might find your problem
in the symptoms table and be able to fix it quickly.

**War Story.** When the TV game I worked on was put into production, the technicians who worked on it came up with their own in-house troubleshooting guide.
The motion of the ball was controlled by the voltage level of a capacitor (i.e., a
tankful of electrons). But the company was buying pretty cheap components and
got a number of leaky capacitors, which were then assembled onto the boards.
The technicians quickly discovered that when the ball moved faster up than down,

capacitor A had to be replaced. When the ball moved faster left than right, capacitor B had to be replaced. They wrote that down and didn't hesitate to replace the appropriate capacitor when there was a ball speed problem. ■

## Where to Get Help

Depending on whether you want insight, expertise, experience, or some combination of these, there are a lot of sources you can turn to. Of course, there are your inside associates—they're smart, they may be experts on a subject, and they may have seen the problem before. Some companies are working on what they call knowledge management systems, which capture information from documents and e-mails, along with the name of the person who wrote them, so that you can look up what your company knows and who knows it. This is brand new stuff as I write this, but it's coming—watch for it and use it if you have it. If you don't have it, you'll just have to find the information the old-fashioned way—by searching your document database and asking the folks around the coffee machine.

If you're dealing with equipment or software from a third-party vendor, e-mail or call that vendor. (If nothing else, the vendor will appreciate the bug report.) Usually, you'll be told about some common misunderstanding you've got; remember, the vendor has both expertise and experience with its product. Sometimes, as in the story about the VGA capture with the broken phase function, the vendor doesn't have experience—you've found a bug its engineers have never seen. But those engineers have the expertise to recognize the problem as a bug and to keep you from banging your head against something you can't fix. They may even give you a fix, or at least a workaround. In the VGA case, the explanation allowed me to compensate, in my code, for their bug.

Consulting the vendor doesn't always mean contacting a service-person. This is impossible with some companies, but most vendors will at least give you some kind of help in written form. This is a good time to reiterate "Read the Manual." In fact, this is where the advice becomes "When All Else Fails, Read the Manual Again." Yes, you already read it because you followed the first rule faithfully. Look at it again, with your newfound focus on your particular problem—you may see or understand something that you didn't before.

Service-challenged vendors often try to compensate by putting information online; look on their Web site for application notes and sample programs. And remember that there are other users with the same problems—find them and ask them for help. Check the Web for resources like user-group message boards. The Usenet newsgroups available at www.dejanews.com or via your Internet service provider are often a wealth of peer-to-peer information. Some of them are even monitored by experts from the vendor, who respond to important questions. As mentioned previously, if you're troubleshooting a common system, look for the appropriate troubleshooting guide.

Finally, there are resources of a more general nature, on tools, programming languages, good design practices, and even debugging. (The rules you've learned in this book will help you apply the information you get from these other sources in a more systematic way.) Go to your local bookstore, hit the online booksellers, subscribe to the relevant magazines and newsletters, and search the Web. Expertise is all around you.

## Don't Be Proud

You may be afraid to ask for help; you may think it's a sign of incompetence. On the contrary, it's a sign of true eagerness to get the bug fixed. If you bring in the right insight, expertise, and/or experience, you get the bug fixed faster. That doesn't reflect poorly on you; if anything, it means you chose your help wisely.

The opposite is also true: Don't assume that you're an idiot and the expert is a god. Sometimes experts screw up, and you can go crazy if you assume it's your mistake.

**War Story.** I was writing a program (a wire-wrap runlist editor in Forth, for you wooden-ships-and-iron-men fans) that utilized a large database-indexing scheme called B-trees. I had started with a code base created by my associate, a computer science jock who used the Knuth book for a pillow at night. At one point, I was working at home reviewing the source code (these were pre-PC days, so I wasn't actually running the code), and I came across a section of his program that I didn't understand. It seemed that in a certain case, the software would drop a whole block of data while rebalancing the tree. I struggled for hours trying to understand what I was doing wrong—the failure seemed too obvious to have escaped the attention of my associate. I had to be missing something.

I finally went into work and spread the listing out on his desk. I told him I couldn't figure out how this would work correctly, and asked him to enlighten me.

He looked at it for a few moments and said, "Hm. That's a bug." ▩

## Report Symptoms, Not Theories

No matter what kind of help you bring in, when you describe the problem, keep one thing in mind: Report symptoms, not theories. The reason you went to someone else for fresh insight is that your theories aren't getting you anywhere. If you go to somebody fresh and lay a theory on her, you drag her right down into the same rut you're in. At the same time, you've probably hidden some key details she needs to know, because your bias says they're not important. So be firm about this. When you ask for help, describe what happened. Describe what you've seen. Describe conditions if you can. Make sure you tell her what's intermittent and what isn't. But don't talk about what you think is the cause of the problem.

Let her come up with her own opinions. They may match yours, or they may, in fact, have that new insight that you went to someone else for in the first place. I've seen this mistake a lot; the help is brought in and immediately poisoned with the old, nonworking theories. (If the theories were any good, there'd be no need to bring in help.) In some cases, a good helper can plow through all that garbage and still get to the facts, but more often you just end up with a big crowd down in that rut.

The doctor you visit for the pain in your lower back wants to hear how it feels, not that you looked it up on the Internet and you're sure you have dorsal cancer. Your auto mechanic wants to know that the engine won't start on cold mornings, not that you think GM built your car on a Monday and some hungover assembly guy overtightened the phineas pin.

This rule works both ways. If you're the helper, cut off the helpee who starts to tell you theories. Cover your ears and chant "La-La-La-La-La." Run away. Don't be poisoned.

## You Don't Have to Be Sure

There's a gray area here. Sometimes you'll see data that smells fishy, looks wrong, or in some way seems to be related to the problem, but you're not sure how or why. This is worth presenting; the fact is, you found something you didn't expect or don't understand. It may not be relevant, but it *is* information. Sometimes, even the pattern of the shirt or the flavor of the ice cream matters.

# Remember

## Get a Fresh View

You need to take a break and get some coffee, anyway.

- **Ask for fresh insights.** Even a dummy can help you see something you didn't see before.

- **Tap expertise.** Only the VGA capture vendor could confirm that the phase function was broken.

- **Listen to the voice of experience.** It will tell you the dome light wire gets pinched all the time.

- **Know that help is all around you.** Coworkers, vendors, the Web, and the bookstore are waiting for you to ask.

- **Don't be proud.** Bugs happen. Take pride in getting rid of them, not in getting rid of them by yourself.

- **Report symptoms, not theories.** Don't drag a crowd into your rut.

- **Realize that you don't have to be sure.** Mention that the shirt was plaid.

## chapter

# 11

# If You Didn't Fix It, It Ain't Fixed

"It is stupidity rather than courage to refuse to recognize danger when it is close upon you."

—SHERLOCK HOLMES, *THE FINAL PROBLEM*

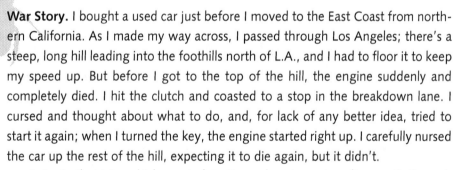

**War Story.** I bought a used car just before I moved to the East Coast from northern California. As I made my way across, I passed through Los Angeles; there's a steep, long hill leading into the foothills north of L.A., and I had to floor it to keep my speed up. But before I got to the top of the hill, the engine suddenly and completely died. I hit the clutch and coasted to a stop in the breakdown lane. I cursed and thought about what to do, and, for lack of any better idea, tried to start it again; when I turned the key, the engine started right up. I carefully nursed the car up the rest of the hill, expecting it to die again, but it didn't.

Later in that trip, which was in late December, I was traveling north through West Virginia; it was a bitter-cold day, with very dry snow blowing, and I stopped at a little mountainside gas station to fill up. Soon thereafter, I was climbing a hill, and again the car stalled. I pulled over, remembering the L.A. incident, and turned the key, and the car started again. I finished climbing the hill and had no more trouble on the trip. Since I didn't really trust the little mountain gas station, I thought maybe it was water in the fuel line (although that wouldn't explain the L.A. problem). I added some Drygas and hoped the problem was gone.

It wasn't. The car stalled again later that winter, on a completely flat road, traveling at highway speed. I pulled over, fumed, and immediately tried to start the car, but couldn't. I fumed a while longer, then tried it again, and this time it started. I was able to drive to work, but I found that whenever I took the speed up above 45 or 50 miles per hour, after a little while the car would stall; then if I sat by the side of the road for a minute or two, it would start again.

Now, I'm not a mechanic, so I took the car to my local auto repair shop. They said, "It's an electrical problem," replaced some wires, and charged me $75. Of course, within a day the car stalled again. (I decided that just because you pay people $50 an hour doesn't mean that they know how to debug something—another early lesson in my engineering career.)

I thought about the incidents. What was common to the situation was that I was flooring the accelerator, either because I was climbing a hill or because I was going fast. After the car stalled, if I waited a while, it would run again. I was familiar enough with engines to know that the engine burns fuel from the carburetor, which has a small reservoir of fuel, which is in turn fed by the gas tank, which is the big reservoir of fuel. I thought that if something restricted the flow of gas from the gas tank to the carburetor, I could easily drain the carburetor when I floored the gas pedal; then I'd have to wait a while for the slow flow of gas from the gas tank to refill the carburetor and let the engine run again (see Figure 11-1).

I then applied the "Get a Fresh View" rule and asked a crowd around the

**Figure 11-1.  A Real Gas Miser.**

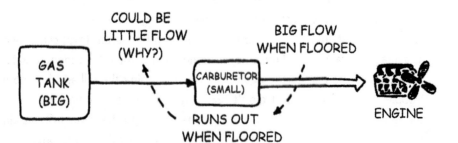

coffee machine at work, "What might constrict fuel flow from the gas tank to the carburetor?" And one of my more knowledgeable friends said, "Dirty fuel filter." I bought a 50-cent fuel filter, replaced it myself, and solved the problem. ▪

The auto repair shop had no idea whether it had fixed the problem. The mechanics there never made it fail and never tested to see that it didn't fail after they fixed it. (They did keep the $75, though. But it was the last dime they got from me.)

## Check That It's Really Fixed

If you follow the "Make It Fail" rule, you'll know how to prove that you've fixed the problem. Do it! Don't assume that the fix works; test it. No matter how obvious the problem and the fix seem to be, you can't be sure until you test it. You might be able to charge some young sucker seventy-five bucks, but he won't be happy about it when it still fails.

## Check That It's Really Your Fix That Fixed It

When you think you've fixed an engineering design, take the fix out. Make sure it's broken again. Put the fix back in. Make sure it's fixed again. Until you've cycled from fixed to broken and back to fixed again, changing only the intended fix, you haven't proved that you fixed it.

"And why not?" you might ask. Because often during debugging you change something that isn't part of the official "fix"—a test sequence or a piece of software or hardware. Maybe just some random factor is different. This is okay if the change has no effect, but sometimes it actually fixes or hides the problem. You don't realize that; you test your fix, and it works. Yay! You go home happy, but your fix had nothing to do with the problem's going away. If you ship that fix to customers who don't get the other changes, it will fail for them. And that's bad.

If the system fails like it used to when you remove only the fix, then you can be pretty sure that the test sequence is right and the fix is indeed what made it work.

A *Sesame Street* episode has SuperGrover and Betty Lou struggling to turn on a computer. Grover says, "Hmm. Maybe if I hop up and down and say 'Wubba!' it'll work." While he hops up and down yelling "Wubba! Wubba! Wubba!" Betty Lou finds the ON button. She pushes it and the computer turns on. Grover, oblivious of Betty Lou's actions, sees that the computer is on and concludes that he has found a valuable computer-repair technique.* ▪

Of course, in situations where you're just fixing a particular device (rather than an engineering design), rebreaking may be unnecessary and inconvenient. There was no need to put the dirty fuel filter back in my car. And putting a heart transplant patient's old heart back in is not only unnecessary and inconvenient, but also dangerous. And silly.

## It Never Just Goes Away by Itself

If you didn't fix it, it ain't fixed. Everyone wants to believe that the bug just went away. "We can't seem to make it fail anymore." "It happened that couple of times, but gee, then something happened

*Included by permission of Sesame Workshop.

and it stopped failing." And of course the logical conclusion is, "Maybe it won't happen again." Guess what? It will.

Assuming that you made it fail earlier, it stopped failing (or just fails less often) because you changed the conditions somehow. If you've been guessing and changing things with a shotgun (tsk, tsk!), you may have even fixed it, but you certainly don't know how, and you probably don't want to bet your next month's pay on its being fixed. You certainly don't want to bet your company's next product on it.

Go back to Chapter 4 and reread how to make intermittent failures happen more regularly. Go back to the original systems and the test scenarios that caused the bug. If you can make it happen with old software but you can't with the latest stuff, you may have fixed it—look at the differences and figure out why.

Sometimes you run out of time. When you have to say, "Boy, that one is too hard to reproduce now; we can't try to fix it," you're not going to sleep as well at night, and sure as shootin', some customer is going to run into the problem and prove that your sleepless nights were justified. So, take advantage of that. Put some instrumentation into the system to capture information if it ever does fail in the field. Then, if it never happens, it never happens, and if it does, you've "Made It Fail" and you have something to look at.

A side benefit is that even if you can't fix it with that information, at least your customers know that you're serious about tracking it down. When they report the problem, it's better to say, "Thanks! We've been trying for months to capture that incredibly rare occurrence; please e-mail us the log file," than to say, "Wow, incredible. That's never happened here."

## Fix the Cause

If a hardware device fails, don't assume that it broke for no reason. If there's a condition that will cause any good part to fail, changing the part will only buy you a little time (if any) before the new part fails too. You have to find the real failure. In the story of the shorted speaker wires at the Christmas party, it was a failure in the wires that caused the fuse in the right channel to blow. Fixing the fuse by replacing it (with the one from the left channel) just blew another fuse. Unfortunately, it was the only other fuse they had.

**War Story.** One of my most disappointing debugging attempts happened when I was still in college. A friend of my family gave me an integrated stereo system, complete with amplifier, AM/FM receiver, and eight-track tape deck. (Yes, it was a long time ago.) But there was a catch: It didn't work anymore; nothing happened when you turned on the power.

I took it to school, got out a meter, and checked the power system. There was no voltage on any of the four or five wires coming out of the transformer, though the power coming in from the switch was good. Bad transformer, I concluded. Of course, not having any documentation, and not having a working transformer, I couldn't tell what voltages were supposed to be coming out, so I couldn't just put in any old replacement. I wrote down the part number of the transformer and ordered a new one from the manufacturer.

Many months later, the transformer arrived. I opened up the stereo and, delighted to find that the wire colors all matched, replaced the old transformer. I turned the stereo on, set it to WBCN (the Boston rock station at the time), and enjoyed the music. I did not measure the voltages on the wires.

An hour or so later, a few of us decided to go visit the WBCN studio (which was in the top of the Prudential building, a few blocks from the frat house) and make a request by holding up a funny sign outside the studio observation window. When we returned, the two guys who stayed behind told us the DJs had commented on the request, and might have played the song. But they didn't know because soon thereafter the stereo started belching smoke and burned out.

Afterward, I removed the burned-out transformer, kicking myself for not measuring the voltages so I could replace it the next time with something easier to get. This time, I *did* measure the circuits that were hooked up to the wires, and

I found that the eight-track deck was shorted. The new transformer didn't have a chance, but it ran long enough to make me think I had fixed the problem.

I never did order another transformer. I threw the stereo out. ■

Obviously, I violated a lot of rules there. I didn't understand the system, and I didn't do enough looking. I thought I was making it fail when I turned on the power switch and nothing happened. I actually made it fail when I tried to drive the short circuit with the new transformer, but I wasn't measuring anything at the time. And that's because, most important, I didn't consider that some other condition might have caused the transformer to fail.

## Fix the Process

Okay, I said I wouldn't get into quality processes, but sometimes the line between fixing a system and fixing the process that created the broken system is hard to spot. And crossing that line may be a good idea. Here's an example: There's oil on the floor of the factory. You could fix it by wiping it up, but the cause of the problem isn't fixed—there's a leaky fitting, and it'll leak some more. So you tighten it. Is it fixed? Nope, it'll come loose again because the machine vibrates too much, and that's because it's held down by only two bolts, instead of four. Whew. Finally, the real oil-on-the-floor bug has been found. You've followed the advice of the previous section and gone after the underlying conditions that created the failure.

Well, no. Because the next machine they install is going to have only two bolts, and . . . and . . . and . . . there's gonna be oil on the floor again. You have to fix the design process to make sure that vibration is properly accounted for in the requirements, design, and test phases.

While we're on the subject of design quality, I've often thought of ISO-9000 as a method for keeping an audit trail of the design process. In this case, the bugs you're trying to find are in the process (neglecting vibration) rather than in the product (leaky fitting), but the audit trail works the same way. As advertised in the introduction, the methods presented in this book are truly general purpose.

# Remember

## If You Didn't Fix It, It Ain't Fixed

And now that you have all these techniques, there's no excuse for leaving it unfixed.

- **Check that it's really fixed.** Don't assume that it was the wires and send that dirty fuel filter back onto the road.

- **Check that it's really your fix that fixed it.** "Wubba!" might not be the thing that did the trick.

- **Know that it *never* just goes away by itself.** Make it come back by using the original Make It Fail methods. If you *have* to ship it, ship it with a trap to catch it when it happens in the field.

- **Fix the cause.** Tear out the useless eight-track deck before you burn out another transformer.

- **Fix the process.** Don't settle for just cleaning up the oil. Fix the way you design machines.

# 12

---

# All the Rules in One Story

"You know my method. It is founded upon the observation of trifles."

—SHERLOCK HOLMES, *THE BOSCOMBE VALLEY MYSTERY*

**War Story.** Company T had a small device that sometimes refused to start up because a microprocessor couldn't properly read from a battery-backed-up memory. Some units were worse than others, and a unit that failed one start-up could work the next time. This meant that the data in the memory was okay—the problem was reading it.

Engineer A attacked the problem and concluded that it was caused by data bus noise of some sort, since the memory was being read incorrectly. The system was a small circuit board containing memory and a battery-backup memory controller, which had been added to an existing main board. The connector between the boards had only two ground pins and one 5-volt pin, so to reduce the noise, the engineer added a thick ground wire between the boards. He also added a capacitor to supply a local reservoir of power on the small board. He wrote up an engineering change order, got it approved, and moved the fix into manufacturing.

Engineer B was called in when the first batch of fixed boards went through manufacturing, and many of them acted exactly the same as before.

Engineer B sat down at nine o'clock in the morning, hooked up a scope to the data lines, and watched what happened when the main board tried to access the memory. When the system failed, the data was not *slightly* corrupted by noise, but was all *1s*. Looking to see what the read pulse looked like, he was astonished to find that there *was no read pulse*. Now, this is a major missing signal problem—not just noise. The microprocessor on the main board was reading and sending a read pulse up to the memory controller chip, but the read pulse was not coming out of the memory controller chip and going to the memory (see Figure 12-1).

**Figure 12-1. The Case of the Missing Read Pulse.**

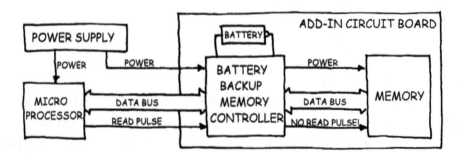

Engineer B quickly consulted the manual and saw that the memory controller chip's job is to prevent accesses (and therefore read pulses) to the memory when the power is not good. This looked promising, but it seemed that nothing was particularly amiss with the power at the time.

At 9:45, the engineer called the manufacturer of the chip and got an applications engineer, who said, "Oh, you probably have a diode between the 5-volt supply and the power supply of the chip; if you do that, it locks into what it thinks is bad power when 5 volts comes up." Sure enough, the design was exactly as the applications engineer had described. (Because the board had been added in later without changes to the main board, the chip maker's recommended design had been modified in what seemed at the time to be a perfectly reasonable way.)

Engineer B needed to attach another wire from the main board to bring in the raw 5 volts as the applications engineer suggested; when he did so, the system worked perfectly. He reversed the fix, saw it fail, put the fix back in, and tested it. It worked fine. Engineer B was done at quarter after ten, really done. (Well, with the fix. Writing up the engineering change order actually took longer than the debugging session.) ▪

Let's review the rules on this one.

**Understand the System.** Engineer A never looked at the data book. Engineer B did, and while he couldn't figure out from the data book why the read pulse wasn't happening, he knew that the chip was the likely suspect, and therefore which vendor he should call. He also knew right away that no read pulse would cause the data to be all 1s.

**Make It Fail.** The fact that the system failed somewhat regularly made Engineer B's job easy. (It also made Engineer A look pretty bad.) Engineer B could see the 1s and the missing read pulse.

**Quit Thinking and Look.** Engineer A never looked at the data, which was all 1s, or the read pulse, which wasn't there. Either one would have quickly shown him that this was not a noise problem.

**Divide and Conquer.** Engineer B looked at the interface and found bad data. He then looked at the memory read pulse and saw that it was missing, so he moved upstream and found the microprocessor pulse going onto the board correctly. This located the misbehaving chip between the good read pulse and the missing one.

**Change One Thing at a Time.** While Engineer B suspected that the other engineer's changes had had no effect, he left them in while he tested—the systems were failing with the changes installed, so he tested with the changes installed.

**Keep an Audit Trail.** Engineer B found no information about why Engineer A thought the problem was noise, or the results of the tests he ran on his fix. Maybe Engineer A kept an audit trail, but he kept it to himself. Manufacturing *did* keep an audit trail; the trouble reports gave perfect evidence that the data in the memory was not bad, since it could sometimes work without reloading the memory. This allowed Engineer B to concentrate on the read function and find the bad data and missing read pulse quickly. The manufacturing test results also clearly showed that the noise fix was not the answer. Engineer B wrote down everything, including the name of the chip vendor's helpful applications engineer.

**Check the Plug.** The chip was acting funny. Engineer B saw no reason for that, and he knew that enough chips were failing that it probably wasn't a bad chip. He questioned whether it was being used correctly, and sure enough, it was a subtle power supply issue.

**Get a Fresh View.** But he didn't *know* if it was being used incorrectly. So he asked an expert. The expert did know, and told Engineer B in a moment.

**If You Didn't Fix It, It Ain't Fixed.** Engineer A obviously didn't test his fix very well, since it didn't work. That embarrassing failure gave Engineer B a really good reason to make sure *his* fix worked before he wrote *his* engineering change order.

# 13

---

# Easy Exercises for the Reader

"What one man can invent, another can discover."

—SHERLOCK HOLMES, *THE ADVENTURE OF THE DANCING MEN*

Can you name *the debugging rules that are at work* or *being violated* in these debugging episodes? (*Hint:* They're in *italics.*) The answers are noted by superscript numbers keyed to the list at the end of each story.

## A Light Vacuuming Job

This is the house-wiring debugging story that I alluded to earlier. It was truly strange, and it gave me an opportunity to get back at my old man for his "when all else fails, read the instructions" comment.

While preparing for a visit from my father to the aforementioned ninety-year-old house in New Hampshire, my wife plugged a vacuum cleaner into a wall socket in the dining room. She told me later that there was something wrong with that socket because *she saw a flash when she turned on the vacuum cleaner.*[1] Curious, of course, *I hooked up the vacuum cleaner, stepped on the pedal, also saw a flash,*[2] and quickly turned it off again. I realized that the flash was not like an electrical spark. It was like—the room lights.

I cautiously *stepped on the pedal again*[3] and, sure enough, the lights in the chandelier over my head came on. The vacuum cleaner, however, did not come on. I found this pretty amusing and decided to *wait until my father showed up to figure it out.*[4] He, of course, was incredulous that any such thing could happen. (He actually used the line *"But that can't happen!"*[5]) We set it up and *proved to him*[6] that, in fact, we could control our chandelier from the vacuum cleaner foot pedal switch.

We thought for a moment about *how the chandelier worked.*[7] The chandelier is controlled by two switches, one at either end of the room. The electricity comes from the main and goes into one switch, which can connect it to either of two wires going over to the other switch. The other switch connects one of those two wires to a common contact on its side, which then goes through the lamp and then back to ground. If the two switches are pointing to the same wire, then the circuit is completed and the light goes on. If you flip either switch so that they're pointing to different wires, there's no connection. Throwing either switch can turn the lamp on or off.

Well, we *guessed*[8] that the plug was probably miswired to that circuit between the two light switches. Sure enough, when we *went down into the basement and followed the wires,*[9] we found two electrical junction boxes side by side, one on the main power and one on the switch circuit. The outlet for the vacuum had been connected to the wrong box, of course, and ended up wired across the two switch lines (see Figure 13-1). When we turned the vacuum cleaner on, it closed the circuit between the switches, turning on the light. But the light used up all the voltage, so there wasn't enough left to turn on the vacuum cleaner motor.

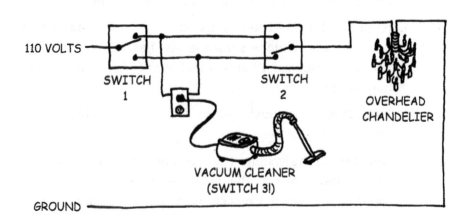

Figure 13-1. A Three-Way Switch.

110 VOLTS

SWITCH 1

SWITCH 2

OVERHEAD CHANDELIER

VACUUM CLEANER
(SWITCH 3!)

GROUND

Wiring in old houses can be pretty entertaining—assuming, of course, that it doesn't burn the house down. ■

The rules, used and (neglected):

1. **Keep an Audit Trail.** She didn't write it down, but what my wife saw was the only significant event of the debugging session. She *did* remember what she saw, though, and didn't just say, "The outlet's broken." She also noticed that only *that* outlet was broken.

2. **Make It Fail.** I took a look for myself and didn't just dive in and rewire.

3. **Make It Fail.** Finding the results of my first test hard to believe, I tested it again. Two failures for two attempts seemed pretty statistically reliable.

4. **Get a Fresh View.** I got my dad involved less because I was stumped than just because I wanted to see the look on his face when I described the problem to him. This is often a good

reason to consult another engineer on a weird bug—it's interesting, and it should be shared with fellow curious people.

5. **(Quit Thinking and Look; Make It Fail).** "That can't happen"
is a statement made by someone who has only thought about
why something can't happen and hasn't looked at it actually
happening.

6. **Make It Fail.** We convinced my dad pretty quickly that it *can*
happen, and did, every time.

7. **Understand the System.** This was a house-wiring problem, so
we examined the way the chandelier circuit worked. Understanding the switches was critical to deciding where to look.

8. **Quit Thinking and Look.** We guessed, but only to focus the
search on the wiring between the switches.

9. **Quit Thinking and Look.** We traced the wires and found the
problem visually.

## A Flock of Bugs

**War Story.** In 1977, we worked on a project that included an unheard-of (at that
time) quarter of a megabyte of memory, which unfortunately did not always read
correctly. One of our software guys *wrote a test program*[1] that loaded memory
with the computer code for the character F (the initial of our company), then
proceeded to read characters out of successive memory locations and *send them
to a video terminal for display.*[2]

These were the days of video terminals rather than PCs. For you youngsters,
a video terminal looks like a PC but has no brains; it simply displays rows of text
characters, filling them in at the bottom of the screen from left to right. When it
needs a new line at the bottom, it scrolls the whole screenful up one line, pushing
the top line off the screen.

It was a fairly fast program, so the characters were streaming at the terminal as rapidly as they could go. Very quickly the entire screen filled with Fs coming in at the bottom and scrolling up to the top. As the lines of Fs shifted up, you couldn't see it, since each line was identical to the one above it. It just looked like a screen full of very steady Fs, even though there was actually a moving field of Fs scrolling rapidly upward through it.

*Whenever there was an error, a different character (V) would appear.*[3] The V would appear at the bottom and very rapidly scroll up to the top. It almost looked like a startled bird taking off and flying straight up (see Figure 13.2).

We *suspected noise problems*[4] in the memory, and one way to make intermittent noise more intense is to touch a finger to the noisy circuit. I *knew which memory chip out of eight to look at*[5] because the character code for F is

**Figure 13-2. Startled Vs.**

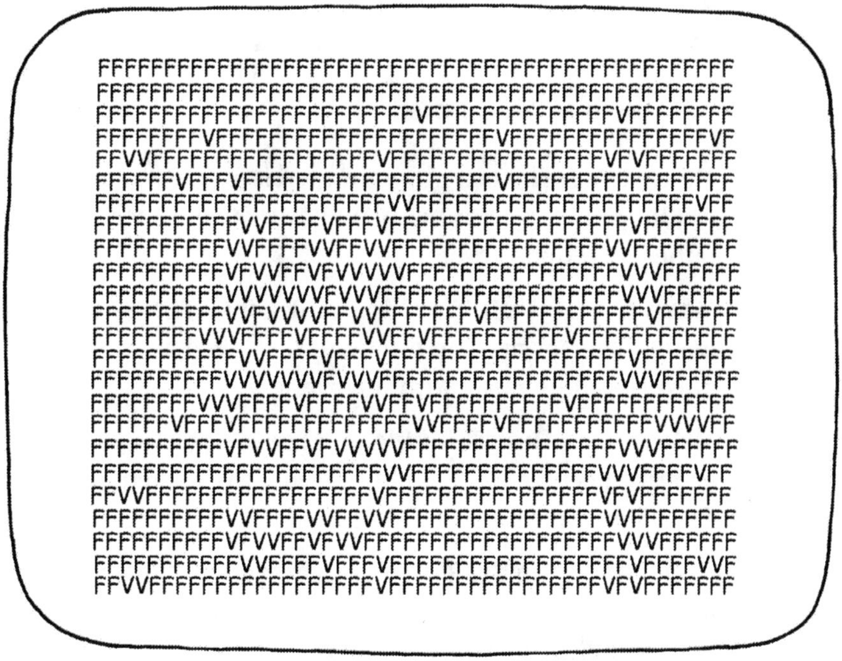

```
FFFFFFFFFFFFFFFFFFFFFFFFFFFFFFFFFFFFFFFFFFFFFFFFFF
FFFFFFFFFFFFFFFFFFFFFFFFFFFFFFFFFFFFFFFFFFFFFFFFFF
FFFFFFFFFFFFFFFFFFFFFFFFVFFFFFFFFFFFFFFFFFVFFFFFFFF
FFFFFFFFVFFFFFFFFFFFFFFFFFFFFFFVFFFFFFFFFFFFFFFFFVF
FFVVFFFFFFFFFFFFFFFFFFFFVFFFFFFFFFFFFFFFFVFVFFFFFFF
FFFFFFVFFFVFFFFFFFFFFFFFFFFFFFFVFFFFFFFFFFFFFFFFFFF
FFFFFFFFFFFFFFFFFFFFFFFVVFFFFFFFFFFFFFFFFFFFFVFF
FFFFFFFFFFFVVFFFFVFFFVFFFFFFFFFFFFFFFFFFFFFFVFFFFFFF
FFFFFFFFFFFVVFFFFVVFFVVFFFFFFFFFFFFFFFFFFFFFFVVFFFFFFFF
FFFFFFFFFFFVFVVFFVFVVVVVFFFFFFFFFFFFFFFFFFFFVVVFFFFFFF
FFFFFFFFFFFFVVVVVVVVFVVVFFFFFFFFFFFFFFFFFFFFFVVVFFFFFFF
FFFFFFFFFFFVVFVVVVVFVVFFFFFFFFFFFFFFFFFFFFFFVFFFFFFF
FFFFFFFFFVVVFFFFVFFFFFVVFFVFFFFFFFFFFFFVFFFFFFFFFFFFFF
FFFFFFFFFFFFVVFFFFVFFFVFFFFFFFFFFFFFFFFFFFFFVFFFFFFFF
FFFFFFFFFFFVVVVVVVFVVVFFFFFFFFFFFFFFFFFFFFFVVVFFFFFFF
FFFFFFFFVVVFFFFFVFFFFFVFFVFFFFFFFFFFFFVFFFFFFFFFFFFFFF
FFFFFFVFFFVFFFFFFFFFFFFFFVVFFFFFVFFFFFFFFFFFFVVVVFF
FFFFFFFFFFVFVVFFVFVVVVVFFFFFFFFFFFFFFFFFFFFVVVFFFFFFF
FFFFFFFFFFFFFFFFFFFFFFFFFVVFFFFFFFFFFFFFFFFVVVFFFFVFF
FFVVFFFFFFFFFFFFFFFFFFVFFFFFFFFFFFFFFFFFFVFVFFFFFFFF
FFFFFFFFFFFVVFFFFVVFFVVFFFFFFFFFFFFFFFFFFVVFFFFFFFFF
FFFFFFFFFFFVFVVFFVFVVFFFFFFFFFFFFFFFFFFFFFFVVFFFFFFF
FFFFFFFFFFFVVFFFFVFFFVFFFFFFFFFFFFFFFFFFFFFVFFFFVVF
FFVVFFFFFFFFFFFFFFFFFFFVFFFFFFFFFFFFFFFFFFVFVFFFFFFFF
```

01000110 and the character code for V is 01010110; clearly the error was in bit 4, which was erroneously coming up 1 when the V appeared. *When I touched a certain group of pins on the memory chip, the screen looked like a flock of birds taking off at the sound of a gunshot;*[6] there were dozens of Vs scrolling up from the bottom of the screen (see Figure 13-2).

*I removed my finger, and it quieted right down.*[7] I then *refined my search;*[8] since my finger isn't very accurate, I took a small piece of wire, held it in my hand, and touched each pin in the group, one by one. I *found the exact pin*[9] that caused the flock of birds and *looked at the signal on it with a scope.*[10] It was a memory control line, and I *saw*[11] nasty ringing on it.

It turned out that the line was too long (the board was 18″ × 24″) and needed a terminator (resistor, not Schwartzenegger) at the end to clean up the signal. *We tested the system for no birds with the terminator, then took it out and saw birds, and then put it back in to verify the fix.*[12] We also *terminated the other signal lines on all of the chips;*[13] since the problem was intermittent on one chip, it might have shown up on the others later. ■

The rules, used and (neglected):

1. **Make It Fail.** The test program exercised the system in a very fast loop, so the error happened every twenty seconds or so, rather than once an hour.

2. **Make It Fail; Quit Thinking and Look.** The test not only made the error happen often but displayed an indication almost simultaneously with the event.

3. **Make It Fail; Quit Thinking and Look.** As well as seeing that an error occurred, we could see what the bad character was. This detail became important later.

4. **Understand the System.** New hardware designs with intermittent errors are often the victims of noise (stray voltages on a wire that turn a 1 into a 0 or vice versa).

5. **Understand the System.** We knew what the computer codes for the characters were, and we knew which memory chip was used to store bit 4. (By the way, for you youngsters, yes, in the old days the really big memory chips were only 1 bit wide.)

6. **Make It Fail.** By introducing additional noise into the system, I was able to make it fail more often. This was a bit lucky, though. For some circuits, touching a finger is like testing that leaky window with a fire hose—the noise will cause a perfectly good circuit to fail. Sometimes the opposite will occur; the capacitance of the finger will eliminate the noise and quiet the system down. (There's a legend that at the analog circuit design lab at MIT in the 1970s, the teaching assistants designed a circuit that was the electrical equivalent of a finger—when they had a noise problem, they would touch various nodes in the circuit until the noise went away, then just solder in the finger circuit to solve the problem for good.)

7. **Make It Fail.** I made sure that my finger was the cause of the burst of errors by removing it (from the circuit!).

8. **Divide and Conquer.** I had narrowed the problem down to four or five pins; now I had to find the exact pin.

9. **Change One Thing at a Time.** I verified that the errors weren't the result of two pins interacting via my finger.

10. **Quit Thinking and Look.** I looked at the signal to find out what was happening. I was assuming noise, but I didn't conclude noise; I just looked.

11. **Quit Thinking and Look.** And I didn't see noise; I saw ringing, which is a different problem, with a different fix. Ringing *does* make the system more prone to noise, which is why it

failed intermittently with the normal noise that was present and why the noise from my finger made it fail even more often. If I had assumed noise and tried to fix it that way, I would have made the problem more sporadic, but it would still have been a problem.

12. **If You Didn't Fix It, It Ain't Fixed.** We made sure that the problem was gone, whether my finger was touching the circuit or not. We also made sure that the problem came back when we removed the fix, again regardless of where I poked my finger.

13. **If You Didn't Fix It, It Ain't Fixed.** We knew that the cause of the failure was bad design, and that the bad design was common to the other signals and chips. We fixed the cause to prevent future problems.

## A Loose Restriction

**War Story.** Our company made circuit boards that turned PCs into videoconferencing systems. Some systems were made up of two boards: one that did audio/video compression and videoconferencing protocols, and another that provided a connection to the communication network. We had two kinds of communication board: one that did ISDN directly to the phone company, and one that did a serial interface called V.35, which would hook up to a customer service unit (CSU), which then hooked up to the phone company (see Figure 13-3). This was great, and we sold both combinations to customers.

We designed a new version of the videoconferencing board using the same communication interface as the old one, so it should have plugged right into the communication boards and worked. But the quality assurance people discovered

Figure 13-3. ISDN Versus V.35.

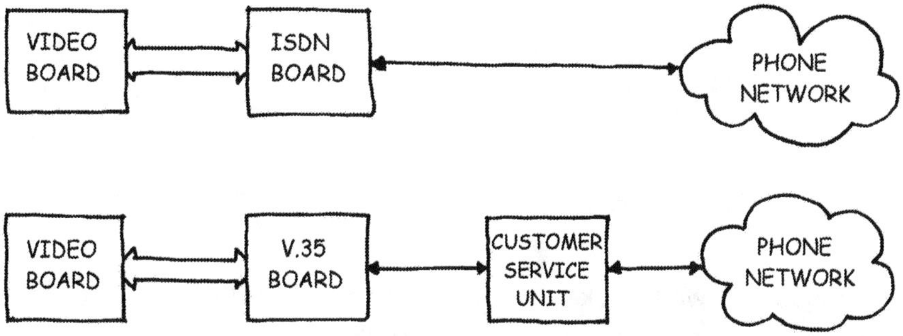

that the new video board couldn't make a certain type of call through the V.35 board. *It failed every time*[1]—not one call of that particular type worked. The ISDN board worked fine.

The calls that failed were restricted calls, a special type of call that allows the phone company to use old, legacy switching equipment. In the old days, the phone company sent calls around the network in 8-bit channels but used one of the bits for internal purposes. The end-point equipment could use the other 7 bits. Modern phone company switches provide "clear channel" calls, so the end point can use all 8 bits. In videoconferencing, we make clear channel calls if we can, but sometimes we can't get a clear channel path because the phone company can only route us through legacy equipment. When that happens, the videoconferencing systems make a restricted call and squeeze everything into 7 bits.

The interface between the video board and the communication board always sends 8 bits, but if the call is restricted, the video board is supposed to use only 7. The V.35 board strips off the unused bit and sends only the good 7 bits to the CSU (see Figure 13-4).

Since the ISDN card worked okay, and the software didn't care what kind of board was hooked up, the software engineers *concluded that the problem must be in the video board hardware,*[2] which had to handle slight differences between the ISDN and V.35 boards. The hardware engineers insisted that since clear chan-

**Figure 13-4. Restricted V.35 Calls.**

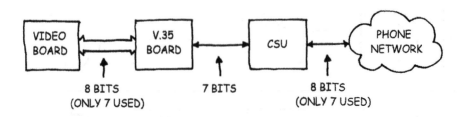

nel V.35 calls worked okay, and the video board hardware acted the same way whether it was restricted or clear channel, the problem *must be in the software.*[3]

The *debug logs told us that the video board couldn't find framing (which was needed to complete the call) in the incoming bits.*[4] One of the software people proved that there was no framing coming in from the hardware by *adding instrumentation on the incoming data buffers.*[5] I was then called in by the software group to find the hardware problem, since I *understood both the video framing protocol and the V.35 hardware.*[6]

I first *confirmed the lack of incoming framing*[7] using the software engineer's data buffer instrumentation. Then I *put a scope on the hardware interface*[8] between the two cards. There was no incoming framing. Then I *looked at the outgoing bits*[9] and was surprised to find the framing on bit 8. This bit was supposed to be unused and was going to get stripped off by the V.35 card, for sure. The framing should have been in bit 7.

We found the function that selects the bit for the output framing and *added a debug log output*[10] every time it was called. We saw the interface getting incorrectly set to bit 8, found the mistaken code that set it, and fixed it; the V.35 card worked fine. *Of course, we removed the fix, saw it fail, and put it back in to confirm the fix.*[11]

The bug had been added as part of the new video card software, which is why the new card didn't work with the V.35 while the old card did. We wondered why the ISDN card worked, as the software indeed didn't care and set the bit wrong in the ISDN case, too. *We confirmed this by looking*[12] at the same intercard

interface with an ISDN card plugged in—the protocol was initially sending framing in bit 8. But after a short while it would move to bit 7.

It turns out that after the protocol has established framing and can communicate with the other side, it sends a command that says, "This is a restricted call."
The other side sees this and responds by moving the framing to bit 7. In the ISDN
case, both sides were getting framing, sending the restricted command, and going
into restricted mode after the initial call was established.

"Wait a minute!" you exclaim. "How did the ISDN card establish framing in
the first place, given that this was a restricted call?" We coolly respond, "*What
makes you think the call was really restricted?*"[13] Our quality assurance department uses an internal switch to provide ISDN service for testing, so we don't pay
any money to the phone company when automatic testing runs thousands of calls
overnight. *Apparently, the switch emulates restricted calls beautifully, doing all
the signaling right, except that it thinks there's no need to actually strip that
eighth bit.*[14] The ISDN card also passes all 8 bits to the emulator (see Figure 13-
5). So the emulator was letting the ISDN system get past the framing problem to
where it could command itself into restricted mode. The V.35, which sends only
the 7 bits, couldn't cheat like that.

I don't know whether any testing had been done on real ISDN lines for restricted mode. But either the testing wasn't done or even the real phone company
transmits the eighth bit if it can, even though it doesn't have to. In either case,

**Figure 13-5. Loosely Restricted ISDN Calls.**

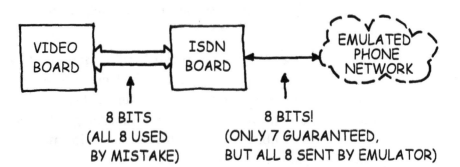

the bug was there, waiting to be discovered. *If the ISDN system had been used in a real restricted phone company circuit, it would have failed just like the V.35 system.*[15] ▪

The rules, used and (neglected):

1. **Make It Fail.** It was remarkably fortunate that we had 100 percent failure. Because this rule was so well served, the problem should have been easy to fix. Missing the other rules made it difficult.

2. **(Quit Thinking and Look).** This is a guess—a bad one, as it turned out, and one that distracted everyone from looking at the problem. It was also the classic finger-pointing.

3. **(Quit Thinking and Look).** The customary retaliatory finger-pointing. This was justified, but there was no way to tell without looking. They didn't look, because the problem was "obviously" not in their area of expertise. That's the worst aspect of thinking-resulting-in-finger-pointing: It actually *prevents* looking.

4. **Quit Thinking and Look.** This bit of looking told us exactly when the system was failing (at the beginning of a call) and what part of the call process was broken. It helped guide our next look.

5. **Quit Thinking and Look; (Divide and Conquer); (Quit Thinking and Look).** One engineer looked, but only to prove that the hardware wasn't delivering framing data to the software. He didn't move upstream to the data going out, which is where the problem was. He *thought* he didn't need to, since he *thought* the hardware was the problem.

6. **Understand the System.** Not only was I familiar with both the hardware and the software, but I had no reason to point the finger at anyone else. (Finger-pointing when there's a problem always amazes me. I *want* the bug in my stuff, so I can fix it. And we're in this together—just because the leak is in somebody else's end of the boat doesn't mean my end won't sink when theirs does.)

7. **Quit Thinking and Look.** I wanted to see the instrumentation for myself, since I knew the protocol better than the engineer who first looked at it.

8. **Divide and Conquer.** He looked at the software that accepted data from the channel. I moved upstream to the hardware interface.

9. **Divide and Conquer.** The incoming hardware stream was bad, so I moved farther upstream. Since this was a bidirectional communication system, I could move up through the V.35 board, through the CSU, through the phone company, through the other side's CSU, and through the other side's V.35, ending up at the interface between the two boards of the other system, except now on the outgoing channel instead of the incoming channel. I confess that I guessed that the problem was symmetrical and looked at the outgoing channel of the system I was near (it had all the connector wires exposed). If it had looked good, I would have actually moved to the other system.

10. **Divide and Conquer; Quit Thinking and Look.** We moved farther upstream to the software that generated the protocol, used instrumentation to see what might be affecting the protocol, and found the restricted mode getting set incorrectly.

11. **If You Didn't Fix It, It Ain't Fixed.** We made sure that fixing the problem routine really fixed the bug.

12. **If You Didn't Fix It, It Ain't Fixed; Quit Thinking and Look.** The nagging question of why the ISDN didn't fail created doubt about the fix. We wanted to understand what was happening to make sure that we had really fixed the problem. So we looked at the ISDN system.

13. **(Check the Plug).** This erroneous assumption was at the heart of the way the problem was originally misdiagnosed. We assumed that the test was valid and that it proved that the ISDN card worked.

14. **(Check the Plug).** The switch people didn't think it was necessary to actually stomp on the eighth bit. They assumed that sending the bit through wouldn't hurt anyone's testing—after all, the unit under test isn't using the bit anyway, right?

15. **(If You Didn't Fix It, It Ain't Fixed).** The need for restricted ISDN calls might have come up and would have caused a failure in the field. It was broken, and we didn't know it. We got lucky.

## The Jig Is Up

**War Story.** We were working on a handheld display with an analog touchpad over the top of it. The touchpad gave the computer two voltage levels, one each for the X and Y locations of the point touched (see Figure 13-6). The pad was not perfectly regular, so the voltages didn't exactly represent positions. We built a

Figure 13-6. A Properly Calibrated Touchpad.

## X, Y VALUES

| 1.1 | 2,1 | 3,1 | 4,1 | 5,1 | 6,1 | 7,1 | 8,1 | 9,1 | 10,1 | 11,1 |
|-----|-----|-----|-----|-----|-----|-----|-----|-----|------|------|
| 1.2 | 2,2 | 3,2 | 4,2 | 5,2 | 6,2 | 7,2 | 8,2 | 9,2 | 10,2 | 11,2 |
| 1.3 | 2,3 | 3,3 | 4,3 | 5,3 | 6,3 | 7,3 | 8,3 | 9,3 | 10,3 | 11,3 |
| 1.4 | 2,4 | 3,4 | 4,4 | 5,4 | 6,4 | 7,4 | 8,4 | 9,4 | 10,4 | 11,4 |
| 1.5 | 2,5 | 3,5 | 4,5 | 5,5 | 6,5 | 7,5 | 8,5 | 9,5 | 10,5 | 11,5 |

calibration mechanism to account for this; we would touch the pad at known positions and measure and store the voltage values; then during operation we would apply some mathematics to figure out how in-between voltages related to in-between positions.

We came up with a mechanical calibration jig that allowed a person to push a stylus through each of five rows of eleven holes. Software recorded the analog X and Y values at each of the touch points. As we worked on our prototypes, we found that the touchpads were inaccurate near the right side, and worse yet at the bottom right corner. We looked carefully at the calculations we were doing during operation, but all of them seemed to make sense.

We also spent some time analyzing the quality and stability of the touchpads, but eventually I *noticed that the pads were wrong instantly after being cali-brated*[1] and, in fact, were *always wrong in the same area, and the error was always toward the top.*[2] I realized that I *didn't know how the calibration algo-rithm worked*[3] and *hadn't confirmed that the calibration was right.*[4]

The next thing we did was just *look at the calibration data.*[5] This was stored in two arrays, first the fifty-five X values, and then the fifty-five Y values. We expected to see the X values start near 0 and increase for eleven samples, then return to 0 and increase for the next eleven, and so on, representing the horizontal values of each of the five rows of eleven points across the pad. That was indeed what we saw.

When we *looked at the Y values,*[6] we *expected to see*[7] eleven values near 0, then eleven higher values, and so on, with each group of eleven values representing the vertical values of one of the sample rows. *What we saw, however, were*[8] ten values in each row that looked correct, but the rightmost value looked like it belonged in the next row (see Figure 13-7). The bottom row had the same problem, but the rightmost value was 0 instead of the proper high number.

We *traced a run of the calibration program,*[9] and the answer jumped right out at us. The programmer had created and named the two arrays, one for the X measurements and one for the Y measurements, and *assumed that the compiler would put them one right after another in memory.*[10] As he got the values during the calibration procedure, he wrote the X value to the proper location, then put the Y value at that location plus 55. (This saved him a line of code, no doubt.)

The compiler, however, decided to locate the arrays on even address boundaries, and so left a space in between the two arrays in memory (see Figure 13-8). As a result, the Y array was 56 bytes after the X array, so all the Y values were placed in the location just before the one in which they should have been stored.

**Figure 13-7. The Improperly Calibrated Touchpad.**

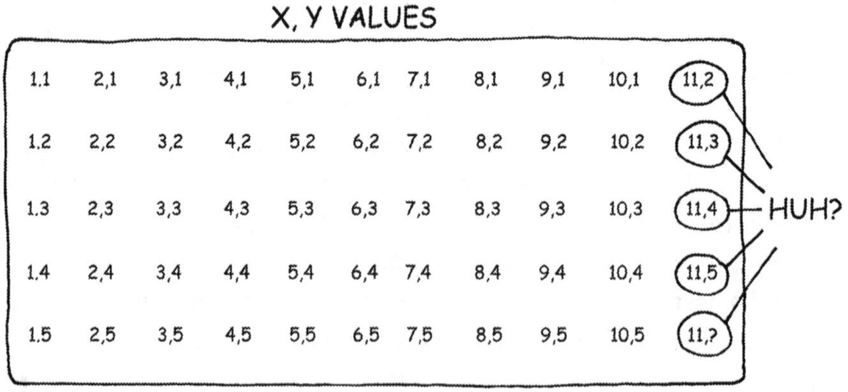

### X, Y VALUES

Figure 13-8.  A Hole in the Theory.

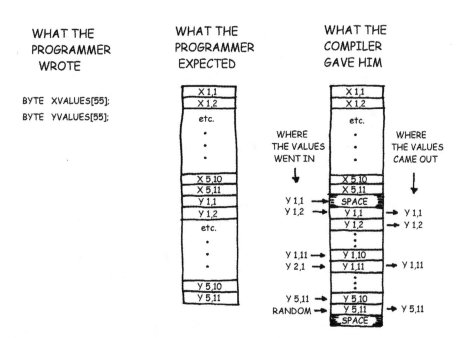

WHAT THE PROGRAMMER WROTE

WHAT THE PROGRAMMER EXPECTED

WHAT THE COMPILER GAVE HIM

BYTE  XVALUES[55];
BYTE  YVALUES[55];

When they were read out, the actual start of the named array was used, so the Y value obtained was always the one just after the intended one.

This was generally fine, because as you worked your way along a row, the Y values were all nearly the same, *and the averaging math that went into the calculation tended to hide the error*[11]—except at the end. Then the Y value clicked over to the next row; the calculation program used the value from the next row at the right edge and got a really wrong answer. In the lower right-hand corner, the Y value (the last one in the array) was never initialized at all, so it came up 0 or some other random value and really messed things up there.

We fixed the calibration algorithm, saw that the touchpads were indeed accurate and stable, *rebroke the algorithm and saw the failure, then refixed it*[12] and sheepishly took back all the nasty things we had said about the touchpad vendor. ▪

The rules, used and (neglected):

1. **Keep an Audit Trail.** We had never really kept track of the calibration error over time, so we assumed that it was drifting. When I first actually tracked it carefully, I was surprised to find that it wasn't drifting, but was wrong from the beginning.

2. **Keep an Audit Trail.** I noted not only the presence of the error, but its location and direction.

3. **(Understand the System).** I didn't know how the algorithm worked, so I never suspected it. Funny how that is.

4. **(Check the Plug).** We all assumed that the calibration was good because most of the points were accurate and we had been assuming that it started off correct.

5. **Quit Thinking and Look; Divide and Conquer.** We looked at the calibration data, which is upstream from the operational program that uses it and downstream from the calibration mechanism that creates it.

6. **Quit Thinking and Look; Divide and Conquer.** We looked at the Y values with great interest, since the error was always in the Y direction.

7. **Understand the System.** We knew what good data would look like.

8. **Quit Thinking and Look.** When you look at something and it doesn't look the way you think it should, you're onto the problem. If you just think, you'll never get that satisfying surprise.

9. **Divide and Conquer; Quit Thinking and Look.** We went upstream again, to the program that generates the data. We instrumented the code and saw the problem.

10. **(Check the Plug).** Here's a great example of assuming something about the tools. This was a very negligent assumption, but it was made anyway, and it was wrong.

11. **(Quit Thinking and Look).** Trying to figure out the problem by looking at the effect of the calibration wasn't successful because the effect was masked by the mathematics, and so the view of what was going on was cloudy. By not looking at the actual data, it was easy to think that the pads were just slightly bad.

12. **If You Didn't Fix It, It Ain't Fixed.** We made sure that the problem was really the calibration and proved that it had indeed been fixed.

# 14

# The View from the Help Desk

"It is always awkward doing business with an alias."

—SHERLOCK HOLMES, *THE ADVENTURE OF THE BLUE CARBUNCLE*

**War Story.** I was dealing with a customer, Giulio, who was in Italy. Giulio was trying to interface our videoconferencing board to someone else's ISDN communication board. He explained to me that the interface on the ISDN board was similar to the interface on our board, but it required some cable changes and a few changes to our programmable protocol hardware. The programmable changes affected whether pulses were positive or negative, which clock edge to sample data on, and other hardware communication things that make for bad data when they're not set right.

We had bad data. Being the expert on the protocol, I was working with him to set the parameters right. He faxed me timing diagrams for the ISDN board, which allowed me to determine the matching settings for our board. After numerous attempts to get them right, hampered by Giulio's limited English (or more fairly, by my nonexistent Italian), I was finally convinced that the settings had to be right. But the data was still wrong. We checked and double-checked the settings and the results. Still wrong. I remember thinking, "This has got to be something obvious that I can't see. It's too bad the videoconferencing isn't already working so I could just look at the system myself, from here."

He faxed me screen shots of his logic analyzer, showing the data just going bad. Since logic analyzers see everything as digital 1s and 0s and can't see noise, I began to suspect noise on the cable. One thing that can help a noisy cable is to make it really short. The following conversation ensued:

Me: "Please make the cable really short, like two inches."

Giulio: "I can't do that."

Me: "Why not?"

Giulio: "I have to leave enough room for the board in the middle of the cable."

Me: "Board in the middle of the cable?!"

As it turned out, the ISDN board put out a fast clock where our board needed a slower one, and Giulio had solved this problem by putting a little circuit board in the middle of the cable to divide the clock in half (see Figure 14-1). The power

**Figure 14-1. Me and Giulio.**

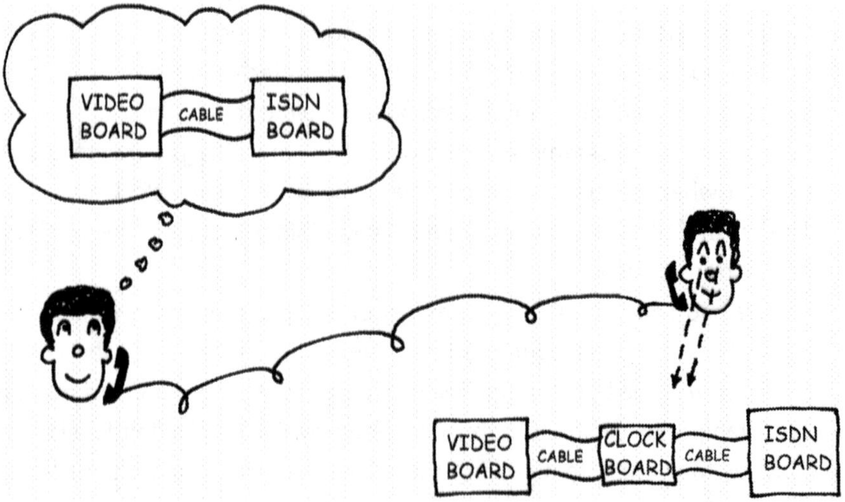

supply noise of this circuit was overloading the limited ground wire on the cable, causing lots of noise. After he rerouted the chip ground away from the cable ground, the two boards communicated happily. ▪

If you work the help desk, you've been in this situation. You can't see what's actually going on at the other end, and you wouldn't guess in a million years the crucial things the users ignore or the crazy things they're willing to believe. You've probably heard the story of the user who complains that his cup holder is broken. After some confusion, the help desk determines that the CD-ROM tray is no longer sliding in and out, probably because of the repeated strain of supporting a cupful of coffee.

Debugging from the help desk has some special issues, and this chapter helps you deal with them.

## Help Desk Constraints

Before we talk about how to apply the debugging rules from the help desk, let's look at why the help desk is not your ordinary debugging situation.

**You are remote.** The rules are a whole lot easier to follow when you can be with the system that's failing. When you're on the phone with the user, you can't accurately tell what's going on, and you can't be sure that the things you want done are being done correctly. You're also faced with new and strange configurations—maybe even foreign languages.

**Your contact person is not nearly as good at this as you are.** The good ones know this—that's why they called you. The rough cases think they know what they're doing, and break it badly before they call you. At a minimum, they tend to jump ahead and do stuff you didn't want done. In any case, they probably haven't read this book.

**You're troubleshooting, not debugging.** At help desk time, the problem is in the field, and it's too late to quietly fix it before release. It's usually something broken (software configuration, hardware, etc.), and you *can* fix it. If it's really a bug (undiscovered until now), you typically can't fix it; you have to try to find a workaround and then report it to engineering so they can fix it later. Of course, the time pressure to fix the problem or find a workaround is enormous, and therefore so is the temptation to take shortcuts.

## The Rules, Help Desk Style

Here we'll go through each of the rules and give you some hints about how to apply them even though the person on the other end of the line thinks his CD-ROM tray is a cup holder. Because no matter how hard they are to apply, the rules are essential, which means you have to figure out a way to apply them.

### Understand the System

When you get a call, the customer has some reason to believe that your product is involved; whether that's true or not, your knowledge of your product is the only thing you can count on. Obviously, that knowledge should be very thorough, including not only everything about the product itself and its recommended or likely configurations, but also its help desk history—previous reported problems and workarounds. You probably know the product better than the engineers who designed it—and that's good.

But, of course, there's other stuff out there—stuff that's connected to, running underneath or on top of, taking all the memory away from, or in some other diabolical way making life miserable for your product. Your primary problem in "Understanding the System" is to find out what that other stuff is and understand it as best you can.

When you ask the customer, you get an opinion, which you can trust only so far. If you have built-in configuration reporting tools, you can get an accurate sense of what's installed and how it's configured. If you don't have those tools, this would be a good time to march on down to the product planning group and pound on their desks until they put configuration reporting tools into the requirements for all future versions of your product.

You can also use third-party tools to get an idea of what's going on—for example, a Windows PC can tell you a lot about what hardware and software are installed, and performance-monitoring tools can tell you what's running and what's eating up the CPU.

When the other stuff is completely unknown to you (like Giulio's ISDN card), try to get information as efficiently as possible—you may not have time to wait for a FedEx of the user's guide, so you have to try to get a high-level working knowledge of what it is and what it does, quickly. Concentrate first on determining the likelihood that it's affecting your problem; then go deeper if it looks like a suspect. This is easy to get wrong, because you can't go deep on everything and you can't always tell that you're missing something important. In the Italian ISDN story, I asked for timing diagrams on the data channels of the card, but I didn't get anything that said there was no appropriate clock. I had no reason to believe there was an additional circuit required, so I didn't pursue that angle. I wasted time because I went deep on understanding the data system and not on understanding the clock system. The moral is, be ready to change focus and dig into a different area when the one you choose comes up innocent.

When the other stuff is hardware, try to get a system diagram as early as possible. If you can get this only verbally, draw your own diagram, and make sure you clearly identify the pieces you're drawing. Make sure the user agrees with these names; it's really hard to make sense of a bug report where "my machine died after talking to the other machine." Even if you have to call things "system A" and "system B," make sure you both have the same clear, unambiguous picture of the whole configuration.

Finally, miswired cables cause lots of strange behavior; if there are any cables involved, get cable diagrams. I only wish I'd asked Giulio for one.

## Make It Fail

When customers call about a broken system, unfortunately, the reason the system is broken is usually a one-of-a-kind series of events. They don't really know what they were doing when it died. The screen froze and they got impatient and clicked all over the place, and then it went crazy. Or, they just came in this morning and it was all screwed up. Or, it looks like somebody might have spilled coffee into it. So while you may get an idea of the sequence that led the system astray, you may very well get a false idea, or no idea at all.

The good news is that, usually, the system is solidly broken. It's easy to make it fail—just try to use it. So even though you have few clues about how it got broken, you can always make it fail and look at what's happening. The fact that the user ran hexedit on the registry file doesn't matter; the error message saying "missing registry entry" will tell you that the registry is broken.

You still have to get a clear picture of the sequence of events that makes the failure *symptom* occur. Start at the beginning; even reboot, if necessary. Carefully identify which systems, windows, buttons, and fields are being manipulated. And make sure you find out exactly what and where the failure is—"The window on the other PC looks funny" isn't a very useful description for the trouble ticket. And when he says, "It crashed," make sure he's not playing a car-racing game.

## Quit Thinking and Look

There are three problems with looking at the failure through the eyes of the users. The first is that they don't understand what you want them to look at. The second is that they can't describe what they see. And the third is that they ignore you and don't look; instead, they give you the answer they assume is true. You're undoubtedly skilled (or should become so) at patiently walking them through the session, repeating steps that aren't clear and suppressing giggles at the things they think you said. ("Okay, now right click in the text box." "You want me to write 'click' in the text box?") But there are two other tools that can help a lot by eliminating the to-err-is-human factor.

Remote control programs, if you have them, put you back in the driver's seat. Screen-sharing programs, even though you can't control them, allow you to monitor what the users are doing in your name, and stop them before they go too far. If these tools aren't a part of your corporate toolbox, maybe you can use a Web-conferencing service to share the user screen via the Internet. Access may be limited by corporate firewalls and other defenses set up by nervous network administrators, but some of these services are fairly transparent if you only have to look at one program at a time. Keep in mind that you will *not* see anything close to real-time performance across the Net; you won't be able to debug that car-racing game.

The second inhuman tool is the log file. If your software can generate log files with interesting instrumentation output, and can save those files, then the user can e-mail them to you for your perusal. (Don't make the poor customer try to read the files—it's hard, and there are often meaningless but scary error messages, or at least a bunch of misspelled words in there.) Remember to follow the rules and keep the files straight (which one was the failure and which one worked), note the times that the error symptoms occurred, *note what the error symptoms were*, and keep all the system time stamps synchronized. These files should also be attached to the trouble ticket, and eventually to the bug report if the problem gets escalated to engineering.

Another issue with looking at a remote problem is that your instrumentation toolset is limited. I was lucky that Giulio had a logic analyzer and could send me traces, but this is not often the case. Even if the users have the tools, they usually can't get into the guts of the system, and if they can, they don't know enough about the guts to figure out where to hook the tool up. On the other hand, if you have somebody like Giulio with a logic analyzer, go for it. Even a simple multimeter can tell you that a cable is wired incorrectly or a power supply is not on.

## Divide and Conquer

Depending on the system, this rule can be either just as easy as being there or next to impossible. The problem is that you're analyzing a production system, so you can't go in and break things apart or add instrumentation at key points to see if the trouble is upstream or downstream. If the instrumentation is there already, great. If intermediate data is stored in a file where you can look at it, great. If the sequence can be broken down into manual steps and the results analyzed in between, great. If you can exercise various pieces of the system independently of the others, great.

If the system is monolithic (from the customer's point of view), that's not great. If the problem is broken hardware, you might just change the whole unit. (Though many a hardware swap has had no effect because no one ever proved the hardware was really at fault, and it wasn't. This is even more annoying if you have to requisition the replacement and ship it to the customer; there's less at risk if the spare part is onsite already.) If it's a real software bug, you may have to re-create the problem in-house so you can modify the code to add the required instrumentation. If it's a configuration bug, you can't re-create it in-house, but you can create a special version of the software and ship it to the customer to get the instrumentation into the places where you need it. A good electronic link to the customer site is very helpful.

Try not to succumb to the temptation to just start swapping hardware or software modules—but if that's the only way to divide up the problem, see the next section.

## Change One Thing at a Time

Unfortunately, by the time you get the call at the help desk, the users have changed everything they can think of, didn't change anything back, and probably can't remember exactly what they did. This is a problem, but there's not a whole lot you can do about it.

What you *can* do is avoid making the problem worse by swapping things in and out in the same way. But as noted in the previous section, sometimes the only way to divide up the system is to replace a file or software module or hardware component and see what changes. In that case, be sure to keep the old one, and be sure to put the old one back after you've done your test.

Sometimes the system is simply hosed, and the only way to get it back is to restart, or reboot, or even reinstall the software. Sometimes you even have to reinstall the operating system. This is the software equivalent of shipping the customer a new system. This will probably work, of course, but any customer data will be lost. If there's a real bug in the system that got you to this sad state of affairs, you've lost any clues you had about that, too. Also, reinstalling the software always looks bad—in the customer's mind, you're grasping at straws. And if this doesn't fix the problem, you've really gone and embarrassed yourself. The one good thing about starting fresh is you have a known base to start Changing One Thing at a Time from.

## Keep an Audit Trail

As a seasoned customer support veteran and a debugging rules expert, of course you write down everything that happens during your help desk session. The only problem is, you don't know what really happened at the customer site. Customers will often do more, less, or something other than what you asked. You have to put some error correction in your conversation.

As you instruct the users to do or undo something, make them tell you when they're done, before you go on to the next step. In fact, have them tell you what they did, rather than just asking them if they did what you asked; that way you can verify that they did the right thing. Many people will answer "yes" regardless of what they did and what you asked—since they didn't understand your request the first time, why would they understand it the second time? Make them tell you what they did in their own words.

Logs and other system-generated audit trails are much more reliable than users, so get and use whatever logs you can. Save them as part of the incident report; they may come in handy the next time the problem occurs, or when the engineers actually get around to fixing the bug you've found. A common problem here is figuring out which log is which, so tell the users exactly what to label everything. Don't trust their judgment on this—instead of two logs labeled "good.log" and "bad.log," you'll get "giulio.log" and "giulio2.log."

Finally, keep digging for information about the situation. Unsophisticated users are very prone to overlook things that are obviously important and that you would never guess. An earlier chapter discussed someone who stuck floppy disks to a file cabinet with a magnet. There's another famous story about a guy who copied data onto a floppy, stuck on a blank label, and then rolled it through a typewriter to type the label. You would never do this. As a result, you would never think to ask if the users did this. All you can do is ask what happened, and then what happened, and then what happened, and so on until they get to the point where they called you.

## Check the Plug

There's an urban legend (maybe true) about a word processor help desk person who gets a call because "all the text went away on my screen." After figuring out that the screen was blank, the troubleshooter told the user to check the monitor connections. This was difficult, said the user, because it was dark; the only light was coming in from the window. As it dawned on the support guy that the power had gone out, he supposedly suggested that the user take the computer back to the store and admit being too stupid to own a computer.

No one is too stupid to own and use your product. And even the smart ones are likely to be in the dark about how your product works and what conditions are needed to make it run. Yes, they will try to install Windows on a Mac. Yes, they will try to fax a document by holding it up in front of the screen. (Okay, those aren't the smart ones.)

The bottom line for you is not to assume *anything* about how the product is being used. Verify everything. And don't let them hear you laugh.

## Get a Fresh View

As mentioned in Chapter 10, troubleshooting guides are very useful when the system is known and the problem has occurred before. You are troubleshooting. Troubleshooting guides are your friend. You should be armed with every related guide you can get your hands on, and that especially includes your own company's product and bug history databases.

Use your fellow support people as well. There may be things they've discovered about the system that they never documented or, more likely, incidents that they never really came to any conclusion about, but that will help shed light on your incident. Of course, they're always at least a fresh point of view and a sounding board to help you clear up your own understanding of the problem.

If you have access to the engineers, they may be able to help, too. Like your fellow support reps, they may know things that aren't documented that can help. They may be able to suggest creative workarounds if you need one. And eventually, they may have to fix the bug—talking with them helps get them thinking about the problem.

### If You Didn't Fix It, It Ain't Fixed

You know you're not going to get off the phone until the user is happy that the problem is fixed. But when the user's problem is fixed, the bug may not be. And even if it is, it may come up again, and you can help.

First of all, contribute to the troubleshooting database. Make sure that what you found gets recorded for the next person who runs into the situation. Try to crystallize the symptoms for the summary, so it'll be easy to recognize the circumstances. And be very clear about what you did so the problem will be easy to solve the next time.

> "An ounce of patience is worth a pound of brains."
>
> —DUTCH PROVERB

If what you came up with was a workaround for a real bug in the system, your user will be happy, but other users are sure to stumble onto the same problem. Enter a bug report, get it into your escalation procedure, and argue that fixing it is important (if, in fact, it is). Don't settle for cleaning up the oil on the floor and tightening the fittings; make sure that future machines get bolted to the floor with four bolts instead of two.

Finally, remember that users are more easily satisfied that the problem has been fixed than a good debugger would be. Invite them to be on the lookout for vestiges of the problem or side effects of the fix. Have them get in touch immediately if anything comes up, so you can get back into it before too many other random changes happen.

# Remember

### The View From the Help Desk Is Murky

You're remote, your eyes and ears are not very accurate, and time is of the essence.

- **Follow the rules.** You have to find ways to apply them in spite of your unenlightened user.

- **Verify actions and results.** Your users will misunderstand you and make mistakes. Discover these early by verifying everything they do and say.

- **Use automated tools.** Get the user out of the picture with system-generated logs and remote monitoring and control tools.

- **Verify even the simplest assumptions.** Yes, some people don't realize you need power to make your word processor work.

- **Use available troubleshooting guides.** You are probably dealing with known good designs; don't ignore the history.

- **Contribute to troubleshooting guides.** If you find a new problem with a known system, help the next support person by documenting everything.

# 15

---

# The Bottom Line

"Has anything escaped me? I trust that there is nothing of consequence which I have overlooked?"

—DR. WATSON, *THE HOUND OF THE BASKERVILLES*

Okay, you've learned the rules. You know them by heart, you understand how to recognize when you're breaking them (and stop), and you know how to apply them in any debugging situation. What now?

## The Debugging Rules Web Site

I've established a Web site at http://www.debuggingrules.com that's dedicated to the advancement of debugging skills everywhere. You should visit, if for no other reason than to download the fancy Debugging Rules poster—you can print it yourself and adorn your office wall as recommended in the book. There are also links to various other resources that you may find useful in your debugging education. And I'll always be interested in hearing *your* interesting, humorous, or instructive (preferably all three) war stories; the Web site will tell you how to send them. Check it out.

## If You're an Engineer

If you're an engineer, programmer, customer support person, or technician, you are now a better debugger than you were before. Use the rules in your job, and use them to communicate your skills to your associates. Check the Web site for new and useful resources, and download the poster. And hang the poster on your wall, so you're always reminded.

Finally, think about each debugging incident after it's over. Were you efficient? How did using (or not using) the rules affect your efficiency, and what might you do differently next time? Which rule should you highlight on your poster?

## If You're a Manager

If you're a manager, you have a bunch of people in your department who should read this book. Some of them are open to anything you ask them to do; some of them are cocky and will have a hard time believing they can learn anything new about debugging. You can put a copy on their desks, but how do you get them to read it?

Assuming they haven't already gotten curious about what the boss is reading, you can get them curious. Download the Debugging Rules poster from the Web site and tack it onto your wall (it's way cooler than those inspirational "teamwork" posters, anyway). Ask them to read the book and give you their opinion—pretend you don't know if the rules really work. They'll either come back fans of the rules or find ways to improve on them, and in either case they'll have absorbed and thought about the general process more than they might have otherwise. (And if they come up with something really interesting or insightful, send it to me at the Web site.)

You can appeal to their sense of team communication. Several of the people who reviewed drafts of the book were team leaders who consider themselves excellent debuggers, but they found that the rules crystallized what they do in terms that they could more easily communicate to their teams. They found it easy to guide their engineers by saying, "Quit Thinking and Look," the way I've been doing for twenty years.

Hey, it's a short, amusing book. Hand them a copy, put them in a room with no phone and no e-mail for an afternoon, and they'll have an enjoyable afternoon at least. (But just to make sure they're not playing games on the Palm, give them a quiz when they're done. And be sure to hide the poster first.)

Finally, remember that once they've learned the rules, they're going to use them to tackle the next debugging task you give them. Don't pressure them to guess their way to a quick solution—give them the time they need to "Understand the System," "Make It Fail," "Quit Thinking and Look," and so on. Be patient, and trust that the rules are usually the quickest way to the fix and will always help keep you out of those endless, fruitless guessing games you desperately want to avoid.

## If You're a Teacher

If you're a technical college instructor, you probably realize that the real-world experiences in these war stories are invaluable to students in the fairly safe world of school projects. You probably also realize that your students will often be the ones called upon to do the heavy lifting in the debugging world—technicians and entry-level programmers have to fix a lot of other people's stuff besides their own. And how well they do that can mean faster advancement and a reputation as a get-it-done engineer. So get them to read it—assign it as required reading and stock it in the school bookstore. You probably don't need a three-credit course for it, but make sure you introduce it at some point in the curriculum—the earlier the better.

# Remember

The rules are "golden," meaning that they're:

- **Universal.** You can apply them to any debugging situation on any system.

- **Fundamental.** They provide the framework for, and guide the choice of, the specific tools and techniques that apply to your system.

- **Essential.** You can't debug effectively without following *all* of them.

- **Easy to remember.** And we keep reminding you:

**The Debugging Rules**

Understand the System

Make It Fail

Quit Thinking and Look

Divide and Conquer

Change One Thing at a Time

Keep an Audit Trail

Check the Plug

Get a Fresh View

If You Didn't Fix It, It Ain't Fixed

Be engineer B and follow the rules. Nail the bugs and be the hero. Go home earlier and get a good night's sleep. Or start partying earlier. You deserve it.

# Index

adoption studies, 86

air leaks, 63

amplification, 33, 35

analyzing the problem, 88–89

assumptions, questioning your, 109–111

audio data problem, 83–84

audit trail, *see* Keep an Audit Trail

automating the process, 29–30

B-tree problem, 121

bad, starting with the, 78–79

beginning, starting at the, 29

bonding, 38–39

brass bar, grabbing the, 88–89

breakout box, 68

cable switching equipment, 73–74

calibration, 150–153

cancer, 62

*Car Talk* (radio show), 40

Carroll, Lewis, on forgetfulness, 105

cause
   fixing the, 129–131
   focusing on the, 27

CD-ROM tray, 159

chandelier problem, 137–140

Change One Thing at a Time (rule 5), 83–95
   and analyzing problem before acting, 88–89
   and changing one test at a time, 89–90
   and comparison to good system, 90–92
   and the help desk, 165
   and using rifle vs. shotgun approach, 85–88

Check the Plug (rule 7), 107–114
   and the help desk, 167
   and questioning your assumptions, 109–111
   and start-up conditions, 111
   and testing tools, 111–114

checksum errors, 45–48

circuit boards, 45–48, 144

clear channel calls, 145

Click and Clack (radio personalities), 40

coffee withdrawal, 100

comments, 14–15
communication errors, 67–68
communications boards, 15–16,
    157–158
communications systems, 60
comparison, 90–92
compression, video, 50–54
conditions
    determination of, 33–34
    start-up, 111
configuration control systems,
    104–105
consistency, 101
consistent data capture, 35–36
constraints on Help Desk, 159–160
control
    of conditions, 33–34
    of variables, 86
correlation, 103–104
CSU, *see* customer service unit
cupholder problem, 159
customer service unit (CSU),
    144–148

damage, limiting the, 29
DD (Drop Dead) instruction, 77
debug logs, 90–92, 163–164, 166
debugging
    rules for, 9–10, 160–169
    troubleshooting vs., 6–7
    Web site on, 171
design changes
    audit trail for, 104–105
    one at a time, 93–94

details, 101–103
    looking up, 21–23
    seeing the, 52–55
    writing down, 105
differencing engines, 90–92
Divide and Conquer (rule 4), 67–81
    fixing the known bugs to, 79–80
    fixing the noise to, 80
    and the help desk, 164–165
    injecting patterns to, 76–77
    narrowing the search to, 71–76
    starting with the bad to, 78–79
documentation, *see* Keep an Audit
        Trail
downstream, 75
Dr. Watson (fictional character), 171
Drop Dead (DD) instruction, 77

eight-track deck, 130–131
Einstein, Albert (on phone books),
    22
electrical shock problem, 102
electrocardiography, 62
engineers, 172
error symptoms, 163
experience, 55, 117–118
experts, 117

failure, *see* Make It Fail
fixes
    of the known bugs, 79–80
    testing the, 27
    *see also* If You Didn't Fix It, It
        Ain't Fixed

floppy disk problem, 99–100
focus
    on the cause, 27
    guessing to increase, 64–66
Forth (language), 121
486 processor reading problem,
    111–112
four-wide telephone circuits, 16
1489A chip, 21–22
frame, phone company, 73–74
framing bits problem, 83–84
frequency of failure, 34
fuel filter problem, 125–127

garbage characters, 104
gas leaks, 63
gauges, 63
Get a Fresh View (rule 8), 115–123
    and the help desk, 167–168
    and reasons to ask for help,
        116–119
    and reporting of symptoms,
        121–122
    and where to get help, 119–120
    and willingness to ask for help,
        120–121
Goldberg's Corollary to Murphy's
    Law, 69
guessing, 64–66

Halt and Catch Fire (HCF) instruc-
    tion, 77
headache problem, 100
heat exchanger problem, 107–109

Heisenberg, Werner, 63
Heisenberg uncertainty principle,
    63–64
help, getting, see Get a Fresh View
Help Desk, see View from the Help
    Desk
hereditary diseases, 62
hot water problems
    in old house, 107–109
    in sink dispenser, 65–66
hotel reservation system problem,
    67–70

ice cream problem, 40
If You Didn't Fix It, It Ain't Fixed
    (rule 9), 125–132
    and fixing the cause, 129–131
    and fixing the process, 131–132
    and the help desk, 168–169
    and intermittent "fixes," 128–129
    and verifying the fix, 127–128
impossible results, 39–41
information, consistent capture of,
    35–36
infrared sensors, 63
initializing variables, 34, 111
instructions, read the, 11–15
instrumentation, 55–63
    adding, when needed, 59–62
    in daily life, 62–63
    design of, 56–59
    system affected by, 63–64
intermittent fixes, 128–129

intermittent problems, 33–39
  consistent data capture with,
    35–36
  observation of, 55
  patterns in, 37
  randomness in, 37–39
intrusive instrumentation, 64
ISO-9000, 132

Keep an Audit Trail (rule 6), 97–106
  of actions, sequence, and results,
    99–100
  and correlating symptoms,
    103–104
  for design and testing, 104–105
  and the help desk, 166–167
  and level of details, 101–103
  of testing procedures, 28
knowing the road map, 18–20
knowing what is reasonable, 17–18
knowing your tools, 20–21
known state, 29

leaky roof problem, 94–95
limiting the damage, 29
lip-synch problem, 77
LISP machine database server, 67
logs, debug, *see* debug logs
looking it up, 21–23
loopback tests, 46

machine state, 29
Make It Fail (rule 2), 25–43
  and the help desk, 162

and impossible results, 39–41
and intermittent problems, 33–39
reasons to, 27
and retaining your debugging
  tools, 41–42
simulating vs. stimulating failure
  to, 30–33
starting at the beginning to, 29
stimulating the failure to, 29–30
managers, 172–173
manual, reading the, 11–15
marker genes, 62
Martin, Steve, on how to become a
  millionaire, 13
metal detectors, 63
microprocessor(s), 18
  486, 111–112
  1489A, 21–22
  Motorola 6800, 77
  for powder-weighing system,
    11–12
  registers for, 14
  slave, 45–48
missing read pulse problem,
  133–135
MIT Innovation Center, 25
mortgage calculation, 86
motion estimation, 53–54
Motorola 6800 microprocessor, 77

narrowing the search, 71–76
natural gas, 63
Nietzsche, Friedrich, on truth, 114
noise, 47, 80

observation, *see* Quit Thinking and
    Look
oil leaks, 131–132

patience, 168
patterns, 37
    injecting easy-to-spot, 76–77
    inserting known, 47
perfectionists, 80
phone books, 22
phone company problems
    with customer service unit,
        144–148
    with switching equipment, 73–74
pixels, 87–88
plaid shirt problem, 97–99
plant growth experiments, 86
plug, checking the, *see* Check the
    Plug
plumbers, 63
pong game, 25–26, 41–42, 118–119
powder-weighing system, 11–12
problem, analyzing the, 88–89
process
    automating the, 29–30
    fixing the, 131–132
programmable gate arrays, 59
prostate cancer, 62
pump problem, 50–51

quantum physics, 63
questioning your assumptions,
    109–111
Quit Thinking and Look (rule 3),
    45–66

of failure, 27
and guessing, 64–66
and the help desk, 163–164
and instrumentation, 55–63
and intermittent bugs, 55
and seeing the details, 52–55
and seeing the failure, 50–52

random data, 34–35
randomness, 37–39
range, target, 71
read problem(s)
    with data, 60
    with processor, 111–112
    with pulse, 133–135
reading everything cover to cover,
    15–17
reading the manual, 11–15
reasonable results, 17–18
reassembly, 69
remote control programs, 163
remoteness (of help desk), 159
reservation system problem, 67–70
results
    documentation of, 99–100
    of failure, 50
    impossible, 39–41
roof problem, 94–95

scientific method, 86
screen-sharing programs, 163
sequence, 99–100
serial interface, 144–148
server computer problem, 51–52

*Sesame Street,* 128
Sherlock Holmes, 1, 9, 11, 25, 45, 67,
    83, 97, 107, 115, 125, 133, 137,
    157
sibling studies, 85
slave microprocessors, 45–48
source code control systems, 104
specifics, 101
stalling, car, 125–127
start-up conditions, 111
starting at the beginning, 29
starting with the bad, 78–79
state of the machine, 29
statistical testing, 37–39
stereo system problems
    with cartridge, 92–93
    with eight-track deck, 130–131
    and fireplace, 89
stimulating the failure, 29–33
submarines, 88–89
successive approximation, 71–72
switching equipment, 73–74
symptoms
    correlating, 103–104
    reporting of, 121–122

target range, 71
teachers, 173–174
testing
    audit trail for, 104–105
    changes to, 89–90
    documentation of, 28
    statistical, 37–39
    of tools, 111–114

text buffer overruns, 104
thermometers, 62
*Through the Looking Glass* (Lewis
    Carroll), 105
timing, 64
tools, debugging
    control of, 105
    keep your, 41–42
    knowing your, 20–21
    testing of, 111–114
touchpad problem, 150–153
troubleshooting, 6–7, 159–160
truth, 114
twin studies, 85–86

uncertainty principle, 63–64
Understand the System (rule 1),
    11–23
    and experience, 55
    and the help desk, 160–162
    knowing the road map to, 18–20
    knowing what is reasonable to,
        17–18
    knowing your tools to, 20–21
    looking it up to, 21–23
    reading everything cover to cover
        to, 15–17
    reading the manual to, 11–15
upstream, 75

vacuum cleaner problem, 137–140
vapor lock, 40
variables
    control of, 86
    initializing, 34

VCRs, 62
vehicle problem(s)
  all-wheel-drive, 28
  with fuel filter, 125–127
  ice cream-related, 40
  with stalling, 125–127
video capture problem, 87–88
video compression problems
  and motion estimation, 52–54
  and plaid shirt, 97–99
video display problems, 62
video resolution, 76
video terminal problem, 140–144
videoconferencing problems
  and bonding, 38–39
  with clock board, 157–158

with customer service unit,
    144–148
  intermittent, 36
view, *see* Get a Fresh View
View from the Help Desk, 157–169
  and constraints, 159–160
  and rules for debugging, 160–169
Volare (automobile), 40
V.35 (serial interface), 144–148

wait time, 16
water heating problems
  with heat-exchanger, 107–109
  with in-sink dispenser, 65–66
Web site (debugging rules), 171

x-rays, 62

# About the Author

Dave Agans is a 1976 MIT graduate whose engineering career spans large companies such as Gould, Fairchild, and Digital Equipment; small startups, including Eloquent Systems and Zydacron; and independent consulting for a variety of clients. He has held most of the customary individual contributor titles as well as System Architect, Director of Software, V.P. Engineering, and Chief Technical Officer. He has played the roles of engineer, project manager, product manager, technical writer, seminar speaker, consultant, and salesman.

Mr. Agans has developed successful integrated circuits, TV games, industrial controls, climate controls, hotel management systems, CAD workstations, handheld PCs, wireless fleet dispatch terminals, and videophones. He holds two U.S. patents. On the nontechnical side, he is a produced musical playwright and lyricist.

Dave currently resides in Amherst, New Hampshire, with his wife, two daughters, and (when they decide to come inside) two cats. In his limited spare time, he enjoys musical theatre, softball, playing and coaching basketball, and writing.

Printed in the USA
CPSIA information can be obtained
at www.ICGtesting.com
JSHW051524010424
60348JS00004B/53

9 780814 474570